DESPERATE FOR
HOPE

Questions We Ask God
in Suffering, Loss, & Longing

Vaneetha Risner

Lifeway Press®
Brentwood, Tennessee

ISBN: 978-1-0877-7504-3 • Item: 005839618
Dewey decimal classification: 234.2
Subject headings: HOPE \ SUFFERING \ JOY AND SORROW

To order additional copies of this resource, write to Lifeway Resources Customer Service; 200 Powell Place, Suite 100, Brentwood, TN, 37027-7707; order online at lifeway.com; fax 615.251.5933; phone toll free 800.458.2772; or email orderentry@lifeway.com.

Printed in the United States of America

Lifeway Women Bible Studies
Lifeway Resources
200 Powell Place, Suite 100,
Brentwood, TN, 37027-7707

Cover painting by Vaneetha Risner
Cover design by Lauren Ervin

**EDITORIAL TEAM
LIFEWAY WOMEN
BIBLE STUDIES**

Becky Loyd
Director
Lifeway Women

Tina Boesch
Manager

Chelsea Waack
Production Leader

Mike Wakefield
Content Editor

Tessa Morrell
Production Editor

Lauren Ervin
Art Director

Sarah Hobbs
Graphic Designer

TABLE *of* CONTENTS

Vaneetha Risner writes and speaks about finding hope in suffering. *Desperate for Hope: Questions We Ask God in Suffering, Loss, and Longing* as well as her memoir, *Walking Through Fire*, encourage readers to turn to Christ in their pain. Vaneetha and her husband, Joel, live in Raleigh, North Carolina, where she blogs at vaneetha.com. She is a regular contributor to *Desiring God* and has been featured on *Family Life Today*, *Joni & Friends*, and *Christianity Today*.

BEFORE YOU BEGIN . . .

Where are you, God? Don't you care that I'm struggling? Why are you letting this happen to me? And why aren't you doing something, *anything*, to help me?

I've whispered, cried, and even screamed those questions to God. I felt so alone in my suffering, distant from God, wondering if my situation would ever change. I asked those questions, not only before I met the Lord but also after I'd walked with Jesus for years. But when my life fell apart, the foundations of my faith felt unstable. The Sunday School answers I could recite automatically made no sense now. I needed something more.

I wanted evidence that God loved me and was with me, that my suffering wasn't meaningless, that this relentless pain wouldn't last forever. Maybe you feel that way too. Maybe you want assurances and real help that is sturdier than what you've relied on in the past.

That's why I wrote this Bible study about the questions we ask God in our suffering. I had questions growing up with a disability, dealing with taunting and hospitalizations. I had questions when my son died after a doctor's mistake, wondering why God let that happen. I had questions when I learned my pain and escalating weakness would never stop, doubting that I could handle it. I had questions when my husband left our family, leaving me to raise struggling adolescent daughters by myself. These events all ignited questions about God—His love, His purposes, and how I would make it through.

Yet in asking these questions, God pushed me into a richer life with Him than I could possibly imagine. Rather than shaking my faith, asking questions confirmed and deepened my trust in God as I learned to live with uncertainty. The more uncertain my circumstances were, the more certain I became that God would never leave me. I would never have to face anything without Him.

Don't be afraid to ask God questions. He invites them.

So what do you want to ask God? Take a minute and write the questions that are currently on your heart. Don't filter what you say. Don't write what you think sounds spiritual. Be honest with yourself and with God. He already knows your heart.

In a similar vein, turn to page 186 and jot down the challenges you are facing right now—the pain, grief, fears, loss, and longings. They don't need to be monumental losses in the eyes of the world, but they can be. Many of our struggles are what my friend calls, "griefs that don't wear black." The losses that aren't on the prayer chain and no one makes a meal for as you deal with them. Childhood wounds. Feeling rejected in friendships. Loneliness. Concern for your children. A difficult marriage. Infertility. Betrayal. A dead-end job. Put everything you can think of on the list. If it matters to you, it matters. And most importantly, it matters to God.

Throughout this study I will talk about three anchors I cling to that have helped me make sense of my suffering. They are the 3 Ps I cling to in pain which remind me there are realities more important than my circumstances. The 3 Ps anchors are 1) Experiencing God's PRESENCE; 2) Knowing my pain has a PURPOSE; 3) Believing the PROMISE of heaven.

These anchors will provide a loose framework focus for the study:

SESSIONS 2–4: PRESENCE
SESSIONS 5–6: PURPOSE
SESSION 7: PROMISE

Through the pages of this study, I'm inviting you into my life. My real life, not the one that looks spiritual and pretty. I've included excerpts from my personal journal—both the raw questions and the ways God answered me. I've also included parts of my Christmas letters that I send to friends each year, in which I share the crazy and embarrassing things our family has said and done.

You may be wondering if you should do this study if you're not currently in a season of suffering. If that's your situation, I think *Desperate for Hope* will be helpful to you for several reasons. First, even if you're not going through trauma, I'm guessing you have things in your life you wish were different. The truths we'll learn in this study apply to everyday struggles as well as life-altering ones. Second, you probably have friends who are facing difficult things. You'll find the kind of encouragement they need in these pages. Third, you may have past losses that you need to process through a biblical lens. You'll find the means and space to do so here. Last, none of us know what tomorrow brings, and suffering may be around the corner for you. I don't say this to scare you but to let you know this study can help prepare you for what might be coming. I am praying that when trials come, you'll turn to God and not away and find that His loving presence will sustain you.

If you are suffering right now, I'm so sorry for your pain. I realize that even starting this study may feel daunting, so just do what you can. You won't magically move through your grief, and all your questions won't be answered in a neat package by the end. But my prayer is that you will encounter God in these pages and that encounter will revive your soul and permanently reshape your heart.

You are beloved.

Vaneetha

Welcome!

This study will attune your heart to the right view of God in suffering and help equip you to walk through your trials with joy and purpose. It will also better prepare you to assist, comfort, and encourage those around you who are walking through difficult times. Because we believe discipleship happens best in community, we encourage you to do this study together in a group setting. Or, if you're doing this alone, consider enlisting a friend or two to go through it at the same time. This will give you study friends to pray with and connect with over coffee or through text or email so you can chat about what you're learning.

HOW TO WATCH YOUR VIDEOS

With the purchase of this book, you have access to teaching videos that provide content to help you better understand and apply what you just studied in the previous session. You'll find detailed information for how to access the teaching videos on the card inserted in the back of your Bible study book.

Here are some things you're going to find in the study:

VIDEO VIEWER GUIDE: As you meet with your group each week, these pages provide a place to take notes from the video teaching and questions to discuss the video teaching. If you're doing the study individually, use the questions for personal reflection.

PERSONAL STUDY: Each week you'll have five days of personal study.

TIME LINE EXERCISE: Toward the back of the study, you'll find pages dedicated to a time line exercise. Instructions for how to use these pages will be provided in the content of the study.

DESPERATE FOR HOPE SCRIPTURE DOCUMENT: Because this study features many Scripture references, we've provided a downloadable document that contains the full text of every Scripture referenced in the study. You can find that document at **lifeway.com/desperateforhope**.

LEADER GUIDE: This downloadable document will help the leader prepare to lead the study and provide instruction for the content and flow of each group session. You'll find this document at **lifeway.com/desperateforhope**.

INTRODUCTION

SESSION 1: VIDEO VIEWER GUIDE

INTRODUCTION

Watch the Session 1 video and take notes below.

GROUP DISCUSSION / QUESTIONS FOR REFLECTION

What part of the video teaching was most significant for you? Why?

Just in the last week, how have you observed suffering taking place around you?

What are some questions you've asked God when you've experienced hardship?

Do you think that at the root we all have the same fears? Same doubts? Same struggles? Explain.

Why is having the right perspective about our suffering so critical?

How has your view of suffering been affected by what you've learned today?

What's one thing you've learned this week of study that better equips you to help others who are suffering?

To access the video teaching sessions, use the instructions in the back of your Bible study book.

Question

IF GOD LOVES ME, HOW COULD HE LET THIS HAPPEN?

DAY 1

I love getting notes and letters, especially from my daughters. When Katie, my oldest daughter, was in preschool, she made me a card that featured her answers to several questions asked by her teacher. One of those questions was "What is your mother's favorite hobby?" I cried when I read her answer: "Making meals for mothers with new babies." I had no idea she even noticed the little things I did. Her card made me feel known and loved.

What makes you feel loved? Is it when someone offers to help without being asked? Or when a friend sends you an unexpected encouraging note? Or when someone notices you're not acting like yourself and invites you to coffee?

When people go out of their way to help us when we're struggling, we know they care. So it's natural to wonder whether God really loves us when He knows our pain yet doesn't rescue us. It's hard to understand how a loving God would allow us to suffer when He has the power to easily remove our trials. It doesn't make sense.

We're going to explore how God could love us and let us suffer, but first, let's talk about suffering in general. I see three major categories of suffering mentioned in the Bible.

1. Suffering because we live in a broken world. Jesus encountered many people who were suffering without any explanation as to why (Luke 7:1-10,11-17).

2. Suffering for the gospel. Paul wrote about the persecution and hardship he experienced for the sake of Christ (2 Cor. 11:16-29).

3. Suffering due to national or personal sin. We see this often in the Old Testament when the Israelites suffered because of their idolatry (2 Kings 17:6-18).

As I read Scripture, all suffering is a consequence of the fall in Genesis 3, which I think is confirmed by Romans 8:20-22. While we often don't understand why we're suffering, if we know Christ, we know that He is using our afflictions for our good and for His glory. For Christians, suffering is always interconnected with God's love.

In the first three weeks we will focus the study around the 3 Ps anchor of GOD'S PRESENCE. We'll start with the story of the raising of Lazarus in John 11, which paradoxically begins with Jesus's absence. This account highlights the questions so many of us have asked, or wanted to ask, and most importantly, how Jesus responds. It is a story about feeling hopeless and abandoned, wondering why Jesus never showed up.

Let's start with an overview of the story.

> **READ JOHN 11:1-44.** Jot down your initial observations. What questions do you have about the text? What resonates with you? What do you notice about Christ's love?

To provide a little background, the only family unit Scripture mentions whom Jesus had a close relationship with is Mary, Martha, and Lazarus. Verse 2 refers to a later event detailed in John 12:1-4 describing a dinner they hosted for Jesus after Lazarus was raised from the dead.

In Luke 10:38-42, we see that Martha welcomed Jesus and the disciples into her home, busily serving them, though distracted and frustrated that she was doing all the work by herself. While Martha was serving, Mary sat listening at Jesus's feet.

Now let's take a closer look at this passage.

READ JOHN 11:1-6. What do we learn about Mary, Martha, and Lazarus from this text?

What verb is repeated in verses 3 and 5 of John 11 that indicates how Jesus felt about the family?

Clearly Jesus loved this family, but He didn't go to them when He first learned that Lazarus was ill. Mary and Martha probably expected Jesus to show up as soon as He heard Lazarus was sick or even to heal him from afar. They probably would have known about, if not witnessed, Jesus healing those in need that He encountered. Acquaintances and strangers. Jews and Gentiles. People who were ill, demon-possessed, and disabled. But He didn't heal His friend Lazarus.

What do you think Jesus meant when He said Lazarus's illness was for the glory of God (v. 4)?

The phrase *the glory of God* is hard to understand. While some scholars admit the phrase is as hard to describe as the word *beautiful*, to me, the glory of God is seeing and marveling at His invisible attributes and His character. When we see God's glory, we know that God is present.

When Moses asked God to show him His glory in Exodus 33:18-23, God said He would cause all His goodness to pass before Moses, and He would proclaim His own name. God would declare His ways, His essence, and character while hiding Moses in the cleft of a rock because no man could see God's face and live.[1] So part of seeing God's glory is experiencing those invisible attributes. When we see

God's glory, we move from mere head knowledge to an intimate experience of God's presence, love, and goodness that grounds our faith.

If you have any other questions about God's glory, write them here. It's an important concept we'll see throughout this week of study.

In the Greek, verse 6 begins with the word *οὖν*, which can mean "consequently" or "so."[2] This means it is connected to the previous sentence. So verses 5 and 6 are linked.

To better understand the link between verses 5 and 6, combine them into one sentence using your own words.

Does Jesus's action, or rather, inaction, surprise you? Explain.

If Jesus responded this way to your suffering, how would you feel? Circle all that apply.

Angry or confused

Unloved, wondering if you were ever close to Jesus

Anxious for an explanation

Tempted to give up on the relationship

Other: _____

_____

_____

_____

While we do not know the specifics of their family situation, we know that Mary, Martha, and Lazarus all lived together. So their loss could have been layered—there would have been a lot to grieve. Missing their brother's daily presence. Potentially losing their income or home. Being afraid of the future. Feeling bewildered and abandoned by a friend.

Mary and Martha had to watch their brother die. Processing our own sorrow is one thing, but seeing the pain of someone else, especially someone we care for, can feel even harder to bear. We can't change their circumstances, change how they're interpreting things, or trust God for them. We can only watch and pray, often feeling helpless.

Perhaps Mary and Martha felt helpless as they watched Lazarus get sick and subsequently die. By not showing up for Lazarus, Jesus had not shown up for Lazarus's sisters. What was Lazarus saying and thinking in his last moments? Did he feel abandoned by Jesus? Were Mary and Martha trying to comfort him, while feeling the very same thing? Did they wonder if their relationship with Jesus was as solid as they once thought?

JOURNAL YOUR RESPONSE TO ONE OR ALL OF THESE QUESTIONS.

Have you ever felt let down by Jesus or watched someone you love feel let down by Jesus? Explain.

Have you prayed earnestly for something, trusting that God would answer you, but the answer you wanted never came? Explain.

Are you waiting now for something from God? Explain.

In John 10, Jesus told the Pharisees that He was the Christ. They considered that blasphemy and wanted to stone Him, but He escaped with the disciples to Bethabara. This place is also known as Bethany beyond the Jordan, where Jesus's ministry began (John 1:28). (For further details, read John 10:22-42.) Bethabara was about twenty miles from Bethany—about a day's journey by foot. Given the time line, it is likely that when Jesus received the news about Lazarus from the messenger, Lazarus was already dead.

Why was Jesus glad that He hadn't been there when Lazarus died (v. 15)?

This first section of John 11 leaves us with heavy questions. We know what it's like to wait for Jesus to fix our situation, to keep waiting and watching, but He doesn't fix it. The answer never comes; God doesn't rescue us. Maybe, like Mary and Martha, our loved one dies. Or we have a wayward child. Or we receive a terminal diagnosis. Whatever it is, our nightmares come true. Perhaps people tell us that it's all for the best, that God will use it for His glory, or that other people may come to Christ through it. But sitting in the midst of our loss, those words can feel cruel and unfair.

Take three minutes and just sit with your feelings about all that has happened thus far in John 11. Feel free to record your thoughts below.

DAY 2

READ JOHN 11:17-27. When Jesus arrived in Bethany, what was happening at the home of Mary and Martha (v. 19)?

In those days, people were buried as soon as they died. Afterward, Jews would (and still do) *sit shiva* for seven days.[3] This meant the family mourned in their home, sitting on the floor or a low bench, receiving visitors who mostly sat in silence interspersed with their tears and moans. Grieving was open and accepted.

How do you handle grief? Circle all the phrases that apply.

Don't talk about it unless asked	Show emotions like tears or anger	Process grief with activity or creativity
Talk about it frequently	Withdraw or pretend it never happened	Other: _____

Acknowledging grief is an important part of healing from a loss. While not everyone processes grief the same way—some internally, others externally—ignoring loss and pretending that it never happened isn't healthy. Yet stoicism is often admired in the Christian community, which implies that grief is a weakness. But in reality, it takes courage and hard work to grieve. Grief is not a frailty of character or a failure to trust God but rather a critical and God-given part of healing. It is the natural and proper response to the loss of something or someone that was loved or valued. It is necessary and can't be ignored.

If there are losses you've never mourned—times of grief you've never processed—record those here. Take a few minutes to journal your thoughts. Grieving is a process, and this is just the first step, so you may need to come back to this later.

When she learned that Jesus was coming, what did Martha immediately do (v. 20)?

Jesus's not coming sooner must have wounded and disappointed Martha, yet she still went to Him as He approached.

I wish my initial response to people when they hurt or disappoint me is to confront them directly. But usually, I'll do *everything but* go to them. I often try to ignore the problem, which can lead to avoidance, while I add to my running mental list (which I regularly review) of how they've wronged me. The relationship then grows distant until one of us is brave enough to start the conversation. Only when I have the courage to tell someone how I feel and hear that person's perspective as well, does our relationship become stronger.

Circle the following areas of life where you have felt hurt or disappointed by God. Briefly describe your experience beside the categories you circled.

FAMILY (MARRIAGE, CHILDREN, PARENTS, SIBLINGS)	
HEALTH	
CHURCH	
RELATIONSHIPS	
CAREER OR FINANCES	
UNFULFILLED LONGINGS/ THINGS THAT WERE NOT WHAT YOU EXPECTED THEM TO BE	
OTHER	

Think about the ways you've responded to people who have hurt you. Compare that to the way you respond to God in your suffering. How has your response to God affected your relationship with Him?

Martha understood doctrine. She immediately affirmed her confidence in Jesus's relationship to the Father, as well as her belief in the Old Testament doctrine of resurrection (vv. 22,24). But Jesus did not want her just to believe in resurrection on the final day; He was also calling her to believe in Him and His power to raise Lazarus that day. He was interested in Martha's proper theology and in her trust and faith.

Verses 25 and 26 are pivotal statements about the gospel. We can be assured of eternal life when we believe in Jesus. He is the resurrection and the life, and if we believe in Him, even when we die, we will live forever. These words applied not only to Mary, Martha, and Lazarus in that day, but to all of us today.

At the end of verse 26, Jesus asked Martha: "Do you believe this?" How would you answer that question?

When life has dealt you a blow, are you like Martha, quick to run to Jesus and express your heart, and then listen for His response? Why or why not?

READ JOHN 11:28-37. What was Jesus's response to Mary
(vv. 32-35)?

Verses 33 and 38 both contain the Greek word *ἐμβριμάομαι* (embrimaomai),
which is usually translated "deeply moved."[4] However, this Greek word literally
means "to snort with anger" or to be moved with indignation. It is similar
to outrage.

Why might Jesus have been outraged at this moment?

Pastor Tim Keller says that Jesus is outraged by death.[5] It is a result of sin, and
Jesus hates its effects in the world He created. Jesus wept with Mary (the Greek
word is literally "shed tears") as He felt her pain over what had happened and
was angry at how death had marred God's beauty.[6] Jesus was not angry because
His friend had died (He would raise him soon) but perhaps at death itself and
all it brings. Death is not domesticated. It's often ugly. Our hope is knowing that
all will one day be made new, but until it is, life can be indescribably hard. And
cause for outrage.

**Are you surprised at Jesus's anger at the tomb? Explain. How can
Jesus's response be comforting?**

Jesus entered into his friends' grief. He knew He would raise Lazarus, and yet He wept with Mary. The sisters had to watch their brother suffer and die, wondering if Jesus would come, while Lazarus experienced the pain of dying. This family that Jesus loved and was intimately connected with was not spared at all.

Anyone who has lost a loved one knows how excruciating that pain is. We shouldn't imagine that it was easier for Mary and Martha. True, Jesus did raise Lazarus from the dead, but that didn't take away the pain of his death. And though we know our loved ones in Christ will be resurrected, the grief of their passing is real. Until Christ returns, we will all experience the full effects of death.

Does the bystanders' question in John 11:37 resonate with you? Explain.

In times of suffering or loss, have you been able to experience God's love and presence? What has that looked like for you? Explain.

What does Jesus's different response to each sister reveal about Him? Do you identify more with Martha who wanted to understand what was happening or with Mary who wanted comfort?

READ JOHN 11:38-44. What strikes you as you read this passage?

Write out verse 40. How is it related to verse 42 and verses 4, 14, and 25-26 from earlier? What is the connection between believing and the glory of God?

John 11 clearly shows that Jesus loved Mary, Martha, and Lazarus. So why didn't Jesus hurry to rescue them from suffering? Why did He wait?

One reason Jesus waited was to reveal the glory of God so that others would believe. While Jesus performed many miracles before this, He hadn't wanted His identity widely known. But now He had begun to openly show who He really was. Furthermore, according to rabbinic tradition, the soul left the body after three days; waiting four days would have emphasized that Lazarus had truly died and was brought back to life.[7] So clearly, raising the dead would be an indisputable miracle to confirm His identity.

While I understand that Lazarus being raised displayed the glory of God, it once seemed heartless to me that a family suffered just for other people to see God. It didn't make sense until I delved into the text. While Jesus's actions brought others to faith (John 11:45), this miracle also solidified this family's faith in Him and deepened their understanding of who He was.

Jesus hated their suffering and hated the pain of death. Yet He knew that after seeing Lazarus raised, they'd trust that Jesus had power over death and would raise them too. And seeing God's glory and believing in Him would be worth all the pain.

Jesus knew that the most loving thing He could do for His friends was to strengthen their faith in Him. So it follows that one of the most loving things God can do for us is to show us more of Himself, even when that involves suffering. My friend Joni Eareckson Tada would agree. Joni is a Christian writer and speaker who became a quadriplegic after a diving accident, has had cancer twice, and lives with relentless, excruciating pain and sleepless nights. She encourages me to press into God in my own pain with the gentle reminder, "The more intense the pain, the closer the embrace."[8] Like Joni, while I wouldn't choose suffering, I've experienced God's breathtaking love and presence in it. Through my suffering, I truly have seen the glory of God.

What have you learned about Jesus through this passage?

DAY 3

We just looked closely at John 11, understanding the passage in its context. Now let's listen to it being read and let the Holy Spirit speak to you through His Word another way.

> **Let's pray:**
>
> *Dear Lord, speak to me through Your Word and show me something of Yourself that I need to see. Help me to clear away all distractions and let Your Word, which is living and active, penetrate my heart that I would encounter You.*

Use an audio Bible app or website to listen to John 11:1-44 being read aloud. (The YouVersion Bible app, Dwell Bible app, the her.bible website, and biblegateway.com are a few options.)

As you listen, put yourself in the story. What phrases do you notice? What do you see? Write anything that speaks to you from hearing the passage.

How has this Scripture affected the way you view your losses and longings?

How do you see Jesus differently from studying this story?

The big question for this week stated a little differently is, *How can God love us and let us suffer?* We wonder why He hasn't rescued us. As we noted yesterday, we understand from John 11 that Jesus didn't rescue His friends so they would see the glory of God and believe in Him. But for most of us, that answer feels unsatisfying—until we experience it.

When I was twenty-weeks pregnant with my second child, during a routine ultrasound they discovered that my unborn son had a rare heart condition that would require surgery at birth. On April 8, 1997, the day we learned of Paul's problem, I wrote in my journal:

April 8, 1997

It will turn out for the best—we just don't know what that is—but You do.

Paul's first surgery went better than anticipated, and I was sure that God had great plans for Paul's life.

When Paul was seven-weeks-old, we took him in for a routine checkup and saw a substitute cardiologist who took Paul off most of his medicine, declaring that Paul was healthy and fine without it. We were thrilled. Yet two days later, Paul screamed in the middle of the night and went limp in my husband's arms. We called 911, but it was too late. Paul was dead.

We were shocked. I wanted to process this pain with God, and I desperately wanted to hold onto Him in this loss.

The day Paul died, my journal entry read:

Please use this for good in my life and everyone's life that knew Paul or even knew about Paul. Give me your comfort because I feel empty inside . . . I just want to scream.

My husband and I spoke at Paul's funeral, declaring that God never makes a mistake. At the time I felt carried by God, but days later I wished I could pull those words back. I wondered why God hadn't spared Paul's life. Why had God let me hope with a successful surgery and then let Paul die in the end? What was the point of faith if God wasn't going to rescue me? My Bible stayed unopened as I pulled away from God, wondering if I could trust Him anymore.

Four months later, I wrote in my journal:

> *I'm glad when people talk about Paul, but it's hard to hear that his death brought them closer to God. Did he have to die for everyone else's good? I feel empty and alone. I ache.*

It bothered me that Paul's life and death brought people closer to God; Paul felt more like a principle, not a person. One day I was aimlessly driving, empty and depressed, and finally asked God to help me. I put on a worship song, and in an instant, the presence of God filled my car. When I turned off the music, the sense of God's presence intensified as I felt surrounded by the glory of God. He was everywhere, and I was overwhelmed by His presence. That moment changed everything—the truths about God's love and comfort that were once academic became breathtakingly real.

Through Paul's life and death, I understood that I was loved and held, but not rescued. I still don't understand why God chose to take Paul when He did, but I do know that glimpsing God's glory anchored my faith.

I told my dear friend, Christa Wells, about my experience with God's comfort amidst my questions and doubts with Paul's death. She encapsulated it in the song *Held*, which was later recorded by Natalie Grant.

The chorus says:

> *This is what it means to be held*
> *How it feels when the sacred is torn from your life*
> *And you survive*
> *This is what it is to be loved*
> *And to know that the promise was*
> *When everything fell, we'd be held* [9]

Write a letter to Jesus, telling Him all that is on your heart. Write your questions. Share your disappointments. Be honest. Talk about the times you've felt abandoned, wondering why He didn't rescue you. Both Martha and Mary began their encounters with Jesus by telling Him, "If you had been here, my brother would not have died" (vv. 21,32). Have you had similar thoughts about your grief and pain? Do you feel Jesus should have responded differently to you? Journal your thoughts.

Turn to your list of current struggles and losses on page 186. Add to that list the hardest events and lowest points of your life with approximate dates. On page 187, begin a list of the happiest moments and high points of your life with approximate dates as well. We'll be using these lists for an important exercise at the end.

DAY 4

My daughters didn't appreciate my input when they were teenagers, particularly when I was reminding them of things I thought they should do. Here's an excerpt from our 2012 Christmas letter:

> *The night before an away basketball game, I listed what Kristi needed to pack. Rolling her eyes, she said, "I got it! Stop bugging me and treating me like a child. I have what I need." Those of you veteran parents are wondering, "So when did she discover something was missing?" The answer is precisely fifteen minutes before the activity bus was leaving when I was out having coffee with a friend.*

While Kristi didn't appreciate that I knew her as well as I did, we all long to be seen, known, and loved.

I moved multiple times before I turned thirty. While I liked the adventure, the first few months in a new place were lonely as I longed to be known. I still remember the first person who invited me to dinner in every city and got to know some of my story. That personal connection changed everything for me.

What makes you feel known? Why is this important?

God knows us better than anyone ever has or ever will. There is nothing about us that God doesn't know. Our fears. Our frustrations. Our fantasies. Our fleeting thoughts and our long-forgotten dreams.

Psalm 139 focuses on how well God knows us. When I visited a close friend who was in the hospital after a mental breakdown, I read Psalm 139 to her, inserting her name as I spoke. She said those words changed her as she understood for the first time that she was fully known, loved, and accepted by God.

READ PSALM 139. **What does God know about you (vv. 1-4)?**

REREAD VERSES 13-16. How does God know us so well? From these verses, what else can you add to the list of what God knows about you?

READ VERSE 17 IN THE TRANSLATIONS BELOW.

"How precious also are Your thoughts **for** *me, God! How vast is the sum of them!" (NASB, emphasis mine).*

"How precious are your thoughts **about** *me, O God. They cannot be numbered!" (NLT, emphasis mine).*

Meditate on this verse for a few minutes and journal your thoughts.

Does this interpretation/translation touch you as deeply as it did me? God thinks about me all the time, and I can't even count His thoughts toward me. They are as innumerable as the grains of sand.

As wonderful as that verse is, you may wonder, as I often have, how God could think about me and everyone else in the world at the same time. But when I read about a video camera that can film at ten trillion frames per second, it made more sense to me.[10] If human beings can make a camera that can process that much information in a second, how much more effortlessly can God know everything we're doing and thinking every second.

God knows us and loves us. We must believe these truths to find real hope in our suffering. Romans 8:31-39 is a stunning passage reassuring us of God's steadfast love, which Paul emphasized through a series of rhetorical questions.

READ EACH QUESTION IN ROMANS 8:31-35, then answer or restate it in the affirmative. I did the first as an example.

◆ Romans 8:31: No one can be against us if God is for us.

◆ Romans 8:32:

◆ Romans 8:33:

◆ Romans 8:34:

◆ Romans 8:35:

READ ROMANS 8:37-39. As you read through the list of what will not separate us from the love of God in Christ, what is most meaningful to you? Why?

READ EPHESIANS 3:16-19. List what Paul prayed for the Ephesians.

Paul was explaining the love of God and asking the Holy Spirit to give the Ephesians strength and power to understand it. That prayer implies we need God's help to know His love; we can't grasp it on our own. Furthermore, Paul uses the Greek word *ginōskō* for *know*, which means "to know by observation and experience."[11] To fully grasp God's love, we need to see it and experience it.

As Christians, we sometimes understand God's love purely intellectually. We know and memorize Scripture, but that can feel disconnected from our everyday lives. God's love is both a fact that grounds our faith and an experience that shapes our lives. It's not just being able to recite Bible verses about God's love but receiving His love in a concrete way. Knowing we are loved is often interconnected with sensing His presence—knowing He is with us. It's not as much a mystical feeling as it is noticing how God shows up for us. In other words, to more fully experience God's love we must be on the lookout for evidence of it.

We may experience God's love in a deep conversation with a friend where we feel understood and known. Or seeing answers to prayer. Or being moved by someone's kindness. When we believe that every good and perfect gift is from above (Jas. 1:17), we can see signs of His love everywhere. Psalm 136 begins with: "Give thanks to the LORD, for he is good, for his steadfast love endures forever" and then recounts how the Lord demonstrates His love to His people. Signs of His love are all around us. We just need to pay attention and specifically ask God to show us how He is loving us.

What are some ways you experience God's love?

Have you ever doubted God's love for you? Are you doubting it now? Explain.

If you were sure that God loved you, how would that change your view of your suffering?

The question: "If God loves me, why did He let this happen?" changes when we are certain that God loves us. It becomes: "*Since* God loves me, why did He let this happen?" This question takes us in the opposite direction of the first one. Now we are looking for a purpose, believing that God has brought these difficult situations into our lives for our good, out of His love for us. That shift in perspective was life changing for me.

God delights in you. God rejoices over you and sings love songs over you (Zeph. 3:17). He couldn't love you more or be more for you than He is right now.

But I recognize that in this moment you may not feel God loves you. While feelings don't define reality, they do frame how we view our lives, our suffering, and our relationships with God. If we don't feel seen, known, and loved, we will come to very different conclusions about what's happened to us. If you are unsure of God's love, reread the Scriptures we studied. Keep praying and asking God to show you that you're beloved. I invite you to pray this prayer with me:

> *Dear Lord, on my own, I can't understand how much You love me, but You can make Your love real to me. Help me understand that in Christ You love me extravagantly and that nothing can separate me from Your love. Please make Your love evident to me this week.*

This excerpt from Jan Richardson's poem "Beloved Is Where We Begin" beautifully states my desire for you.

> *Do not leave*
> *without hearing*
> *who you are:*
> *Beloved,*
> *named by the One*
> *who has traveled this path*
> *before you.*
>
> *Do not go*
> *without letting it echo*
> *in your ears,*
> *and if you find*
> *it is hard*
> *to let it into your heart,*
> *do not despair.*
> *That is what*
> *this journey is for.*[12]

Beloved is where we begin.

DAY 5

We started this week asking the big question: *If God loves me, how could He let this happen?* Has this week's study helped answer that question? Explain.

How have you experienced God's love and faithfulness toward you this week? Where have you sensed His presence? Pay attention to signs of His love and presence through specific incidents like answers to prayer, unexpected peace, comfort after reading Scripture, and so forth.

How is God working in you? In your suffering?

READ PSALM 31:7. What do you see in this verse and what have you learned this week about being seen, known, and loved?

Is God's love more intellectual or experiential for you? Explain.

How has the Lord comforted you in your sorrow and difficulties over the last days and weeks? Where have you seen evidence of His love? Thank Him for that now.

Elisabeth Elliot said, "God never withholds from His child that which His love and wisdom call *good* . . . God's refusals are always merciful—"severe mercies" at times but mercies all the same."[13] She also said, "God never denies us our hearts desire except to give us something better."[14]

What are your thoughts about these statements? Is it more comforting or confusing? Explain.

Read the following statements. Choose one, look up the verse, write that verse on a sticky note or note card, and put it in a prominent place to remind you of God's love.

God delights in me.
READ PSALM 18:19.

God cares about every detail of my life. He keeps track of my sorrows and collects all my tears.
READ PSALM 56:8.

Even when it looks like everything is falling apart, I can count on God's love.
READ ISAIAH 54:10.

God is for me. He will always give me what is best.
READ ROMANS 8:31-32.

Nothing will ever be able to separate me from God's love.
READ ROMANS 8:38-39.

Final Thought

On page 20, I asked you to journal about anything you might be grieving or need to grieve. Grief can feel like a roller coaster, which is natural. It's rarely worked through all at once or resolved in a neat package. **Set aside a few minutes to reflect on your loss and how you could process it further.** Consider praying and meditating on verses we studied this week. Journal about your experience. Consider going to counseling, talking through it with friends, or joining a group like GriefShare® as future options. Or perhaps engage through non-verbal ways like music, art, taking a walk, sitting in the sunshine, cooking, or physical activity. Don't bottle it up or suffer in silence. Take the steps you need to take to allow the Lord to heal your brokenness.

Bonus Study

On page 15 we talked about the glory of God and on page 14 we tied God's love to His glory.

Does that make sense to you? Write any questions you have about it here.

Read the following Scriptures about the glory of God. How do they add to your understanding of God's glory?

- Exodus 33:17-23; 34:1-8

- Exodus 40:34-38

- Luke 9:28-36

- John 1:14-18

- John 2:11

SESSION 2: VIDEO VIEWER GUIDE

IF GOD LOVES ME, HOW COULD HE LET THIS HAPPEN?

Watch the Session 2 video and take notes below.

GROUP DISCUSSION / QUESTIONS FOR REFLECTION

What part of the video teaching was most significant for you? Why?

Have you ever wondered if Jesus really cares for you? If so, why?

Why does suffering sometimes push us away from God and sometimes push us toward Him?

What are some ways God has shown and continually shows His love for you?

How does knowing that Jesus also suffered help you in your suffering?

How has your view of suffering been affected by what you've learned today?

What's one thing you've learned this week of study that better equips you to help others who are suffering?

To access the video teaching sessions, use the instructions in the back of your Bible study book.

Question

HOW CAN I KNOW GOD'S PRESENCE WHEN HE FEELS SO DISTANT?

DAY 1

My children don't listen to me. Most of the time, my stirring mini-sermons or insightful questions fall on deaf ears as they sigh and say, "not another life lesson." When they were younger, they apparently couldn't even hear some of my direct requests. Here is an excerpt from our 2008 Christmas letter:

> *Like many kids, Kristi has selective hearing—capable of repeating our whispered conversations verbatim, but seemingly impervious to direct instructions. One day, feeling exasperated, I questioned Kristi about her delayed response, Kristi replied, "But, I only heard you the third time you called me, Mom."*

I'm thankful that, unlike my children, the God of the universe is always listening to me. He hears me every time I call to Him, and He responds.

Remember that the 3 Ps anchors I cling to in suffering are giving us a framework for the study. This is the second of three sessions that are focused on the anchor of God's PRESENCE. Last week we looked at the love of God, and how, in His love for us, He always gives us what is best. We are seen, known, and loved by Him who is with us in our trouble—even when He doesn't rescue us from it. This week we will see how the disciplines of reading the Bible and praying can usher us into the presence of God where we ultimately find our greatest joy.

Let's start by talking about prayer.

Prayer is an incredible gift from God, but it sometimes feels more like a chore than a grace.

When you struggle with prayer, which statements describe how you feel? Circle all the obstacles that are true for you.

I wonder if God is listening because nothing is happening. Prayer doesn't seem to make a difference.

I'm not sure God can change the person or situation. It seems impossible.

I don't want to pray. It takes too much effort.

I don't know how to pray or what to ask.

Other

_____

_____

_____

Let's look at Hannah, the mother of the prophet Samuel, whose story gives us a beautiful example of a type of prayer we use in suffering: lament.

READ 1 SAMUEL 1:1-20. Jot down your initial observations. What do you notice about Hannah's relationship with God?

Now let's take a closer look.

REREAD VERSES 1-8. What do you learn about the relationship between Hannah and Peninnah? Between Hannah and Elkanah?

Who closed Hannah's womb? What are your thoughts and feelings as you read that?

We will see how God used Hannah's barrenness for good, but we don't see why He chose to do it that way. For years, Hannah probably did not see any purpose to her pain as she wept before God. Perhaps you've also felt that way.

Peninnah's cruel taunting, coupled with her many children, would have magnified Hannah's grief over not having a child. In verse 7, we see that whenever the family traveled to Shiloh to worship the Lord, Hannah ended up weeping and not eating. Perhaps you understand that pain as you long for children or to be married, and you can't handle opening another shower or wedding invitation. Or perhaps you long for deep friendships, a loving spouse, believing children, financial security, a healthy body, or a "normal" family (however you'd define that), and it's just not materializing. You may feel frustrated seeing people who have what you long for and seem to take it for granted. You may wonder, as I have, *Why can't it be me?*

Like Hannah, perhaps going to church where everyone looks cleaned up and perfect intensifies your pain. I know I'm more aware of what's missing and messy in my life when I'm surrounded by people whose lives seem so tidy.

What do you think was the most painful part of Hannah's suffering? Where can you relate to it?

How did Elkanah try to comfort Hannah (vv. 5,8)? How do you think that made her feel?

Have you tried to comfort someone by telling them to count his or her blessings? Has anyone ever tried to comfort you that way? What was the result?

Have you ever overlooked your blessings and solely focused on what you're missing? Choosing gratitude can sound trite, especially in suffering, but how can it be helpful? Have you ever written a gratitude list? What were the results?

READ 1 SAMUEL 1:9-18. Summarize what Hannah did in her pain (vv. 9-11). Include where she went, what she did, and what she said to God.

How do you handle your pain? What does that process look like for you?

I love Hannah's example of going directly to God with her distress—pouring out her heart, her hurt, and her requests.

What did Eli assume about Hannah, and how did he respond to her? If you were Hannah, how would you have reacted? What can you learn from Hannah's example?

What do we learn about Hannah's heart and attitude from her interaction with Eli?

In verse 16, Hannah stated that she was praying out of her "great anxiety and vexation" ("depth of my anguish and resentment," CSB). The Hebrew words used to describe her prayer were *siakh* and **kaas**. *Siakh* means *complaint* and *kaas* can be translated as *grief, wrath, indignation,* or *anger*, particularly at unjust treatment.[1] So she was offering complaint and angry tears to the Lord.

Do you think it was appropriate for her to pray that way? Explain.

Have you ever prayed that way? What was the result?

Where do you go when you are sad, anxious, or discouraged? Do you go to social media, zone out in front of the TV, or vent to a friend? Or do you go to God with your pain as Hannah did? We call Hannah's anguished prayer to God *lament*, pouring out unedited emotions and pain to God. Lament is a way to process strong emotions, to grieve with hope, expressing outrage at our loss while trusting in God's goodness.

Candidly complaining to God does not reflect a weak faith but rather a deep trust in Him. Lament is a direct turning to God, refusing to turn away from Him, even in our grief and disappointment. It is working out our struggles with God. *With* Him. Lament declares we are putting our hope in God even when our struggles feel painful and pointless. Our vulnerability with the Lord brings us directly into His presence, which is what we most deeply need in our suffering.

As we see from Hannah, lament doesn't always need audible words.

READ ROMANS 8:26. Note what it teaches us about wordless prayer. How is that verse encouraging to you?

Sometimes we can't even put our anguish into words. Thankfully, when that happens, the Spirit will pray on our behalf, knowing what we need. Groanings from the Spirit is powerful prayer.

When Eli realized that Hannah was a righteous woman praying from a broken heart, he too wanted God to grant her request. But her situation was unchanged when she left the temple.

What was Hannah's response to both Eli's words and her time with the Lord (v. 18)? Why do you think her face was no longer sad?

READ 1 SAMUEL 1:19-20; 2:1. What did Hannah do before they left for home (v. 19a)? What can you learn from her example?

What was the result of Hannah's prayer? (vv. 1:20; 2:1). List all the reasons for her joy.

Hannah's outlook changed after her lament, even before her prayer was answered. The same can be true for us. Telling God how I feel in my anguish has brought me into a mysterious and extraordinary sense of God's presence. I've left changed, almost undone. Through lament, God has led me to unprecedented times of intimacy and joy with Him.

After Hannah's lament, God remembered her; He answered her prayer, and she gave birth to a son.

Hannah was discouraged and wept for many years as she waited and prayed for a child. She may have had the same struggles with prayer that you do—wondering if God was even listening to her, if He could change the situation, or if it was even worth the effort to pray.

How can being honest about your grief lead you to a deeper faith in God than pretending you're okay? Are you honest with God about how you feel? Explain.

DAY 2

Part of lament is complaining, which I have no problem doing (with God or anyone else), but I'm not so excited when my children complain. Here's an excerpt from our 2004 Christmas letter:

> As many of you know, we try to teach the girls using the Bible, and I'd been working with Katie on being thankful and not complaining. They had memorized Philippians 2:14, and one day I asked her to repeat it. Katie responded, "Do nothing without complaining or arguing." Enough said.

I may get tired of my children's complaints, but I am thankful that God never tires of hearing from us. As David modeled in Psalm 142:2, we can pour out our complaints before God and tell Him our troubles.

But how else should we pray when we're suffering? Can we ask God to remove our suffering, or should we just pray for the strength to endure it? Jesus's prayer in the garden of Gethsemane has helped me answer that question.

READ MARK 14:32-40. Jot down your initial observations. What stands out to you?

READ MARK 14:32-34. How was Jesus feeling? What did Jesus directly ask Peter, James, and John to do? What, if anything, is surprising to you in this passage?

I love seeing the humanity of Jesus here. He knew how the story would end, but He was deeply distressed about what He was about to face. He knew He'd be betrayed, denied, mocked, and beaten. He also knew He'd be forsaken by and out of communion with the Father as He endured a horrific death. Before He started that painful journey, Jesus asked His friends to be with Him.

Have there been times of struggle when you wanted friends to be with you? Did you ask them to come or simply wish they knew what you needed? Explain.

Jesus called on "Abba, Father" in His prayer (v. 36). Why in suffering is it particularly important to remember that God is our Father? How can that influence your prayer life?

It may be difficult to think of God as your Father because of the harsh or abusive treatment you received from your earthly father. Please know that God the Father is not like that. He loves you deeply and tenderly (1 John 3:1). He has adopted you and called you His own (Rom. 8:14-17). You can trust Him.

What did Jesus say is possible for God (Mark 14:36)? Do you believe this is true? If not, stop and ask God to give you the faith to believe (Mark 9:24).

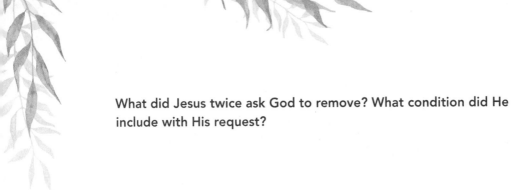

What did Jesus twice ask God to remove? What condition did He include with His request?

Have you ever thought it was wrong or unspiritual to ask God for healing and better just to ask God for strength? Explain. How does Jesus's prayer show you how to pray?

What do you want to boldly ask God for? Stop and ask Him now.

What might God be calling you to relinquish to Him?

What did Jesus want the disciples to pray for and why (v. 38)? Where have you found that your spirit is willing but your flesh is weak?

In Gethsemane, Jesus told His disciples to watch and pray so they wouldn't enter into temptation.

How can you pray about situations and thought patterns that derail you during the day? Why is that important?

At the beginning of this week on page 42, we identified a few obstacles to prayer. While we've learned about prayer in suffering from both Hannah's and Jesus's examples, I'm including additional Scriptures and thoughts that have encouraged me.

For the main obstacles to prayer you identified on page 42, read the corresponding section. Choose two to three associated Scriptures and write truth(s) you want to remember.

OVERCOMING OBSTACLES TO PRAYER

I wonder if God is listening because nothing is happening. Prayer doesn't seem to make a difference.

When I pray and don't see results for a long time, I often assume nothing is happening. But I've learned to trust that God is working and will give us His best in due time. Like Chinese bamboo, which shows minimal growth for the first five years as it builds an extensive root system and then erupts up to ninety feet in five weeks, God may be getting ready to show us His answer.[2] But even if our requests aren't answered as we prayed, we can be assured that God is listening and responding to our cries (Ps. 10:17; Isa. 30:19; Jer. 33:3; Dan. 10:12; Mic. 7:7; Matt. 18:19-20; Luke 18:1).

TRUTHS TO REMEMBER:

I'm not sure God can change the person or situation. It seems impossible.

When I realize that God created the universe with a word and can call into existence things that do not currently exist, I pray bolder prayers (2 Kings 6:15-18; Ps. 78:12-16; Prov. 21:1; Jer. 32:17,27; Luke 18:27; Heb. 11:3).

TRUTHS TO REMEMBER:

I don't want to pray. It takes too much effort.

You don't need to muster up desire on your own. You can say, "Lord, I don't feel motivated to pray. Help me want to." We need to recognize we're in a spiritual battle and that Satan wants to keep us from praying. Our prayers don't need to be "spiritual;" they need to be honest. Prayer can be as short and simple as "Help me" (Matt. 6:7; Eph. 6:12; Jas. 4:2b,7-8; 1 Pet. 5:8-9).

TRUTHS TO REMEMBER:

I don't know how to pray or what to ask.

When I don't know what to pray, I borrow the words of others. I pray Scripture. The Lord's prayer is a great guide, especially when you intersperse it with your own words and requests (Neh. 1:4-11; Ps. 6; 51:1-4,9-12; Matt. 6:5-15; Luke 18:9-14; Eph. 1:15-23; 3:14-21).

TRUTHS TO REMEMBER:

What have you learned in this day of study that you're going to apply to your own prayer life?

DAY 3

We just looked closely at 1 Samuel 1:1-20, understanding the passage within its context. Now let's listen to it being read and let the Holy Spirit speak to you through His Word another way.

> Let's pray:
>
> *Dear Lord, speak to me through Your Word and show me something about Yourself that I need to see. Help me to clear away all distractions and let Your Word, which is living and active, penetrate my heart so that I would encounter You.*

Use an audio Bible app or website to listen to 1 Samuel 1:1-20 being read aloud. (The YouVersion Bible app, Dwell Bible app, the her.bible website, and biblegateway.com are a few options.)

> As you listen, put yourself in the scene. What phrases do you notice? What do you see? Write anything that speaks to you from hearing the passage.

> How has this Scripture affected the way you view lament in your losses and longings?

> How do you see the Lord differently from studying this story?

After I became a Christian in high school, I was excited about growing in my faith. I read Christian books, got involved in a campus ministry in college, and led a small group. I thought I had the Christian life figured out. But after college, I drifted from God as I immersed myself in my career and the lives of my non-Christian friends. When I did open the Bible, it was out of obligation. And each time it felt drier and more boring.

Then my life fell apart. In almost every way possible. In desperation, I opened the Bible and started talking to God. Really talking to Him. I'd spent almost a decade being content listening to good sermons, getting advice from friends, and reading devotionals. But suddenly that wasn't enough. I needed something solid to hold onto, and I found it as I met God in Scripture.

I learned to lament after Paul died; I saw that honesty and tears brought a stunning intimacy with Jesus. I learned to pray and study Scripture when I taught it. During that time, I also witnessed miraculous answers to prayer. I learned to love the Word when my husband left us, and I was desperate for God to draw near. I wanted God's wisdom and comfort, and I needed His Spirit to point out my sin. Only then could I repent and be refreshed by God's presence (Acts 3:19-20) and transformed by Him.

My journal entry from August 16, 2009, shows how the Lord did all those things.

I got up early yesterday morning and mentally went over all the ways Dave wronged me. The more I pondered it, the angrier I got. After a while of stewing in my anger, I realized I hadn't fixed my eyes firmly on Christ. My eyes were fixed on myself.

I thought of Peter. He could walk on water when his eyes were on Jesus. But when he took his eyes off Jesus and focused on the external, he started to sink. Right now I am in over my head. The waters are deep and I will drown in them. I cannot do this by myself.

But as I read the Word and pray, little by little I see myself being transformed. The weight of the burdens falls off. I feel a huge lightness. As I meditate on the Word, it is like balm to my soul. And I have a new perspective as I see Your truth. As I study

Psalm 119, I am reminded that the Word revives us. It gives us life. We fade without it—wilt as flowers in the hot sun—but the Word of God restores us.

Psalm 119, which contains 176 verses about God's word, had always felt dull and repetitive. Yet in this new season it ministered hope and encouragement. Portions of it became part of my vocabulary and are still part of my vocabulary today. I wanted God to show up for me; I wanted to see something in the Scripture I was reading. So I would pray "open my eyes, that I would see wonderful things in your law" (Ps. 119:18) every morning, and somehow God would meet me. As I repeated, "My soul clings to the dust; revive me according to your word," (Ps. 119:25, NASB). God revived me.

I discovered that reading the Bible and prayer are entwined as Scripture informs our prayers. God speaks to us through His Word, and we respond to Him. That exchange has given me joy in God's presence (Ps. 16:11), even amidst crushing sorrow. Just as lament begins with complaint and tears but ends with trust and praise, my time in the Bible transformed me. I tasted the goodness of God (Ps. 34:8), and His words became more precious than food. I understood Jeremiah's joy when he said: "Your words were found, and I ate them, and your words became to me a joy and the delight of my heart" (Jer. 15:16).

The Bible teaches us how to lament. Over one third of the psalms are considered laments where the writers candidly brought their questions, fears, and doubts before God. They boldly complained, asked for deliverance and relief, and somehow moved to genuine trust and praise through the encounter. The same happens with us. We don't need to manufacture the turn from complaining to trust; it occurs naturally as we shift our focus from ourselves to God, which remarkably ushers us into His presence.

Psalm 13 demonstrates the four elements found in most prayers of lament:

1. Turning to God

2. Complaining

3. Asking for help

4. Choosing to trust and praise

We will use the format of Psalm 13 to write our own lament.

REREAD PSALM 13:1-2. This psalm of lament combines the first two elements—turning to God and complaining.

Write your own complaints and questions to God below.

Where are you, O Lord?

REREAD PSALM 13:3-4. The psalmist asked God for deliverance, telling God what he wanted.

Write your own requests to God below.

Lord, will you . . . ?

REREAD PSALM 13:5-6. David concluded the psalm by trusting and praising God, even though his situation was unchanged.

Write your own words of praise and words of trust in God below.

But You, O God, are . . .

Other psalms of lament that can be good models for prayer are Psalms 6; 42; 77; and 142. Psalm 77 helps us remember God's past faithfulness, trusting that He will continue to be faithful.

DAY 4

Since this is a Bible study, most of you reading these words probably believe the Bible is important and helpful. But have you found life and joy in the Scripture? Maybe studying Scripture as your go-to answer book has only increased your knowledge, or perhaps it's just another thing to do on your long list of obligations.

> **What role has Scripture played in your life? Has that role changed over time? Explain. At what times in your life have you read the Bible most diligently? When has your reading and studying been most intermittent?**

I understand that sometimes opening the Bible when you're struggling is hard. You may feel too overwhelmed to get out of bed, much less to read anything. Or you may have an overflowing schedule that makes it challenging to find dedicated time for study. Satan wants to keep us from Scripture by convincing us that reading the Bible is just another chore. And your motivation to read can be greatly influenced by what you want to get out of it.

> **So, what do you want to get out of reading the Bible? Do you identify with any of these good, biblical reasons for reading the Word?**

- To learn what Scripture says so I can follow it (Ps. 86:11; 119:33)

- To grow as a Christian and to see myself clearly (2 Tim. 3:16-17; Heb. 4:12)

- To get wisdom, counsel, or practical advice (Ps. 32:8; 119:24)

- To be instructed, encouraged, and comforted by its words (Ps. 119:76; Rom. 15:4)

- To meet God, know Him more deeply, and delight in Him (Ps. 16:11; Jer. 15:16)

We do gain these wonderful things from reading the Bible, yet knowledge of Scripture doesn't always lead to life change. The Pharisees were well-versed in Scripture, but their hearts remained hard. They knew Scripture, but they didn't know God (John 8:19) or His power (Matt. 22:29), so their knowledge ultimately meant nothing (John 5:39-40). As a result, they resisted the Holy Spirit (Acts 7:51).

WHY WE NEED GOD'S HELP TO READ THE BIBLE

Reading and knowing Scripture is not the end goal. The end goal is to know God, that we would delight in Him. We can get practical advice, comforting words, doctrine, and knowledge from the Bible without interacting with God. But to find joy in the Word and in God, to treasure Him and be transformed, we need God's help (2 Cor. 3:18). The Bible is a supernatural book, and we need God's Spirit to help us understand it (1 Cor. 2:12,14). The Spirit makes God's Word come alive, transforming the words on a page to become life for us.

We read the Bible to see, savor, and be transformed. Seeing is a gift; not everyone who reads Scripture can see what's there—only God can supernaturally reveal it to us. Only then does the Word ignite our hearts as it did for those disciples traveling to Emmaus after Jesus's resurrection (Luke 24:32,45). Seeing like that leads to savoring God—where His joy becomes ours. Finally, this seeing and savoring God's glory transforms us.

The process begins with God opening our eyes but requires our careful observation as we apply the text to our lives. It means simultaneously relying on God and asking for wisdom as we open the Bible and read attentively. It is both a natural and supernatural act.

When Peter declared that Jesus was the Christ, the Son of the living God (Matt. 16:16), he hadn't heard from God directly as John the Baptist had at Jesus's baptism (Matt. 3:17), but the revelation was supernaturally inspired. Jesus responded, "Blessed are you, Simon Bar-Jonah! For flesh and blood has not revealed this to you, but my Father who is in heaven" (Matt. 16:17). Like this revelation to Peter, only God can reveal the truths of Scripture to us. Because of that, we need to approach Scripture with a sense of helplessness and a reliance on God. We must ask God to help us and trust that He will.[3]

BEFORE YOU READ THE BIBLE

The acronym WORD represents what I want God to do in me as I read Scripture. You might find it a helpful reminder of what to pray before you read the Bible, especially when you add words to make it your own.

W – Waken my ears to listen to Your voice.

O – Open my eyes to see Your wondrous truth and understand it.

R – Reveal my sin and Your ways.

D – Direct my heart to Your love and to worship.

The following is an explanation of WORD and what's behind it.

READ EACH SECTION AND THE CORRESPONDING VERSES.
Then in the blank, write in your own words, specifically what you are asking God to do.

W – Waken my ears to listen to Your voice.
The Bible is the primary way that God speaks to us, but to hear His voice, we need to listen attentively.

1 Samuel 3:9 • Isaiah 50:4

Lord, would You _____

O – Open my eyes to see truth and understand it.
We need God's help to see the wondrous truths in Scripture and to understand what they mean.

Psalm 119:18 • Luke 24:45

Lord, would You _____

R – Reveal my sin and Your ways.
We cannot see our sin or know the ways of God until He reveals them.

Psalm 25:8 ◆ Hebrews 4:12

Lord, would You _____

D – Direct my heart to Your love and to worship.
Our Scripture reading should result in rejoicing in God's love and worshiping Him.

Psalm 119:76-77 ◆ 2 Thessalonians 3:5

Lord, would You _____

HOW TO READ THE BIBLE

Here are three practices that can help your Bible reading become
more meaningful:

1. Pay Attention to What the Text Says

To know God, we need to know what His Word says. Look into it long and
carefully. Don't passively drift through the text. Memorize passages, note
surprising words or phrases, and rewrite Scripture by hand to help you see what's
there. Moses saw the value of rewriting Scripture and even instructed Israel's
future kings to recopy the law for themselves to help them learn to fear God and
obey Him and so they'd always have it (Deut. 17:18-20).

2. Dig Until You Understand the Meaning

Each book in the Bible was written to a specific audience, so we must first read
with that context in mind, and then discern what it means for us. Don't dismiss
the things that you don't understand but rather keep digging, not putting
yourself "over" the Scripture, assuming it has to fit your view but instead put
yourself "under" it and let it shape you.

3. Respond to Scripture

Obey what God says in His Word since we are to be doers of the Word and not hearers only (Jas. 1:22). As we saw in Nehemiah 8, the scribe Ezra encouraged those who heard the words to serve those who were not prepared for their holy celebration.

Essentially, these instructions are encouraging us to look at Scripture and ask:

- What does it say?

- What does it mean?

- What do I do?

A BIBLICAL EXAMPLE OF INTERACTING WITH SCRIPTURE

READ NEHEMIAH 8:1-12. Who listened to the Scripture being read? What did they do as it was being read (vv. 3,5-6)?

What did Jeshua and the other Levites do (vv. 7-8)? Why was their work important? Why is this kind of work important now?

What did the people do first after they heard God's Word (v. 9)? Have you ever mourned or grieved after reading the Bible? If so, why?

What did Ezra and other leaders encourage the people to do and why (vv. 10-11)?

How did the people respond to this encouragement (v. 12)? When have you experienced joy reading and understanding God's Word? If that's not the typical experience for you, ask God to show you what's hindering your joy. You may need to confess, repent, and be obedient to God's leading.

WHAT SPENDING TIME WITH GOD CAN LOOK LIKE

We have the privilege of talking to and listening to the God who created the universe and controls everything in it. But we still often struggle to carve out time with Him, especially in an overwhelming season. And when we don't have any desire to meet with God, sometimes the first step is simply asking God to help us want to read the Bible and talk with Him.

Listed below is how I structure my personal time with God. Please don't see this as the be-all and end-all template for what to do. In fact, in different stages of my life, this looked very different!

Your time with God doesn't need to follow a certain format. Find what works best for you.

My PERSONAL TIME WITH GOD

- *I go to bed early* because sleep is the biggest factor in both my consistency and attentiveness in the morning.

- *I minimize distractions,* not checking my phone before I start OR while I'm reading. However, if I do get distracted, I stop and ask God to help me refocus.

- *I use a physical Bible* so I can write in the margins and underline.

- *I journal* in lined notebooks. I may write about the events in my life, how I'm feeling, my interaction with Scripture, or my prayers. It can be just a few sentences.

- *I keep a scratchpad by my Bible* to jot down my random thoughts that often later get folded into my to-do-list.

- *I decide what I'm studying beforehand* and have it ready each morning. If you're new to Bible reading, consider starting with a gospel and reading a section each day.

- I ask God to help me as *I read the Word using the WORD prayer* (page 59).

- *I expect God will show me something* and read with that in mind. Rather than rushing to finish what I'm reading, I think about the passages' implications and applications.

- *I talk to God as I read*—praising Him, repenting, making requests as I interact with the passage.

- *I pray* using notecards. I've created a praise card with attributes of God and a repentance card with sins I'm struggling with. Then I have daily prayer cards for my family and weekly prayer cards for friends, those who are suffering, people in ministry, and others. I adapted this method from the book, *A Praying Life* by Paul Miller.

We began this week asking how we can know God's presence when He feels distant. It starts with talking to God, believing He is listening and answering our prayers. It is honestly lamenting, knowing that our cries will lead to joy. It is reading and studying His Word. The goal of prayer and reading Scripture is not accumulating more knowledge; it's encountering God—seeking His face, hearing His voice, enjoying His presence, worshiping Him, and beholding His glory. Those things will transform us. Undoubtedly Scripture does many other things; it gives us hope, revives our hearts, teaches us God's ways, comforts us with His promises, and gives us wisdom, to name a few. But our reading should ultimately lead us to God Himself. And in deep suffering, more than anything else, our hearts need to experience His presence. As we begin to view all of life through the lens of God's presence, we'll discover that even in our sorrow we can find fullness of joy in Him.

DAY 5

We started this week asking the big question: *How can I know God's presence when He feels so distant?* Has this week's study helped answer that question? Explain.

How have you experienced God's love and faithfulness toward you this week? Where have you sensed His presence? Pay attention to signs of His love and presence through specific incidents like answers to prayer, unexpected peace, and comfort after reading Scripture.

How is God working in you? In your suffering?

READ PSALM 63:1-8. How do these verses reinforce truths from this lesson?

Rewrite the acronym WORD and try to remember what each letter stands for. If you need to, go back and reread that section and the corresponding Scriptures.

W

O

R

D

What does it look like to delight in God? Have you ever experienced that? Explain.

These are some of my go-to Scripture verses that have become part of my vocabulary. They are about joy, God's presence, and what I often ask God to do.

Choose one statement, look up the verse, write it out on a sticky note or note card, and put it in a prominent place. Constantly being reminded of this truth will help you find joy in the Lord and the Word.

God shows us His ways and gives us joy in His presence.
READ PSALM 16:11.

We can taste and see the goodness of God as we run to Him.
READ PSALM 34:8.

God will show me wonderful things from His Word as I seek Him.
READ PSALM 119:18.

God will revive me with His Word when I'm completely discouraged.
READ PSALM 119:25.

God's Word is a delight and joy for those who know Him.
READ JEREMIAH 15:16.

Final Thought

I once wondered whether immersing myself in Scripture actually made a difference. I thought maybe people enthusiastically recommended it just to sound spiritual. Perhaps you've wondered that as well. It wasn't until I tried it myself, committing to time with the Lord every day, that I found how life-giving a relationship with Him can be. If you are struggling in your walk with God and He feels distant, sit with God in silence for a few minutes and then ask Him for motivation to read the Bible and pray. If you're suffering, write out a personal lament as we did on Day 3. Or choose a few Scriptures we studied this week and meditate on them, asking the Lord to reveal Himself to you through them.

HOW CAN I KNOW GOD'S PRESENCE WHEN HE FEELS SO DISTANT?

Watch the Session 3 video and take notes below.

GROUP DISCUSSION / QUESTIONS FOR REFLECTION

What part of the video teaching was most significant for you? Why?

Why does God often feel distant in our suffering?

How would you describe or define lament?

Why is it so important for us to be able to lament in our suffering?

How have you found comfort and help through prayer and the Scriptures in difficult times?

How has your view of suffering been affected by what you've learned today?

What's one thing you've learned this week of study that better equips you to help others who are suffering?

To access the video teaching sessions, use the instructions in the back of your Bible study book.

Question

WHAT IF THE WORST HAPPENS?

DAY 1

Greg broke my heart when I was in my early twenties. We had been dating for a while, and I thought we were going to get married—until he called one night and broke up with me. He didn't give much explanation except to say he didn't feel the same way anymore. We talked several times afterward as I tried to piece together what had happened and salvage our relationship. But I couldn't.

After processing Greg's rejection, I began fearing the worst. Was something wrong with me? Would anyone ever love me again? Had this been my only chance at happiness?

I couldn't imagine a future with someone else and didn't want to. But as I sought God, He put my wounded heart back together. I didn't feel assured that I'd find someone else, but I did sense that even if I remained single, God would be enough. I longed to be married, but even if He didn't fulfill that dream, I knew God would never leave me and that He would fulfill His purpose for me. Knowing that brought a flood of peace.

This week's study completes our 3 Ps focus on God's PRESENCE. We begin by looking at the women near the cross during Jesus's crucifixion. I'm sure, in the moment, they thought the worst was happening.

READ JOHN 19:23-27. Who was at the foot of the cross with the soldiers?

Let's take a closer look at two of the women mentioned in the passage.

READ LUKE 1:26-33. How did Gabriel greet Mary and what was his message to her?

What five things did the angel tell her about Jesus (vv. 32-33)?

If you were told all this by an angel, without knowing the end of the story, what would you expect your life to be like?

Mary's life was filled with a mixture of joy and pain. Let's look at both categories.

First, Mary's joy, promise, and reassurances were unmistakable. She probably had big dreams for her life.

- Mary was favored by God and told she would bear God's Son (Luke 1:30-32). She had reassurance of the angel's promises from:

  » Her cousin Elizabeth who recognized Jesus in the womb (Luke 1:39-45)

  » An angel who appeared to Joseph in a dream (Matt. 1:20-25)

  » The shepherds who witnessed the angels' proclamation of Jesus's birth (Luke 2:8-20)

  » Simeon and Anna, who recognized the newborn Jesus in the temple (Luke 2:27-38)

  » The wise men who traveled from afar to meet the new King (Matt. 2:9-10)

- Jesus was obedient and submissive to His parents (Luke 2:51-52).

But Mary's pain, loss, and disappointments were intense and unexpected, especially given the promises.

- Mary was a betrothed virgin; her pregnancy could have brought shame and the threat of stoning if it was thought to have been the result of an adulterous affair (John 8:3-5).

- Joseph, her betrothed, questioned her character and wanted to divorce her quietly (Matt. 1:19).

- She traveled a far distance, pregnant, with only Joseph at her side (Luke 2:4-5).

- Her newborn baby was laid in a manger—a feeding trough for animals (Luke 2:6-7).

- Simeon, who recognized Jesus in the temple, told her that a sword would pierce her soul (Luke 2:35).

- Mary and Joseph were poor; they offered turtledoves, not a lamb, at Jesus's dedication (Lev. 12:8).

- Mary was at the foot of the cross, watching her Son die alongside criminals.

What are your thoughts as you read through both lists? Did anything surprise you? Trouble you? Explain.

Have you ever thought your life would go smoothly because you were following Jesus? As a young Christian, I was convinced that God would bless me with a pain-free life because I was serving Him. I wonder if Mary had similar thoughts.

Mary knew that Jesus was the Son of God, who would sit on the throne of David. Did she wonder when His reign would begin? When Jesus told her "My hour has not yet come" at Cana (John 2:4), did she wonder when His hour would come? As Jesus hung on the cross, did Mary wonder what happened to all the promises God had made? Or wonder how being favored by God could possibly end this way?

What do you think Mary's unique loss and longings might have been as she saw Jesus on the cross? Are there elements that you can identify with? Explain.

What would you say to a Christian who said all suffering was punishment from God? How does Mary's story contradict that idea?

The other woman at the cross we'll look at is Mary Magdalene.

READ LUKE 8:1-3. What do we find out about Mary Magdalene in this passage?

In Mark 5:1-20, we see a man possessed by multiple demons that tormented him, forcing him to wander alone in the tombs. No one wanted to go near him. Though not all demon-possessions were the same, perhaps his story reveals something of the life Jesus rescued Mary Magdalene from.

Years ago, I witnessed an incredible change in someone I love. But I often feared that the change was temporary and her life would return to the difficulties she had before. Maybe you've had a similar experience—you or someone you love was rescued by Jesus, but you wondered if that rescue would last.

In addition to losing her Rescuer, Mary Magdalene may have wondered what would happen to her when Jesus died. Did she wonder if her nightmarish past of demonic terror would come roaring back? Did she worry about what would become of Jesus's followers, who were perhaps her first real friends and real community? Think about these things as you answer the following question.

What do you think Mary Magdalene's unique loss and longings were as she stood watching the crucifixion? Where can you identify with her?

Imagine you were with these women at the foot of the cross as Jesus took His last breath and darkness descended on the land. A small group huddled together, perhaps feeling abandoned by those who fled. Yet they stayed until the end, with their eyes on Jesus.

READ LUKE 23:54-56; 24:1. How did the women display their love and devotion to Jesus?

These women never left Jesus, following His body to see where He was buried. Once they knew His resting place, they went home to get everything ready for His burial. Despite their grief, they still acted.

I understand that. Even when you're heartbroken, you still have to make dinner. The kids still need to get to school. There are piles of laundry, bills to pay, countless things to be done. In this case, the body needed to be prepared for burial—a process that required spices to deal with the decay.

There were so many things to do after my son Paul died, I didn't know where to start. Elisabeth Elliot, whose husband Jim Elliot was martyred on the mission field, was well known for her admonition to "do the next thing" even in the middle of grief.[1] Which is what I did. I had to tell loved ones what happened. Plan a funeral.

Write an obituary. Pick out a casket. It felt overwhelming, yet as I kept doing the next thing, I was able to move forward.

> **How can the phrase "do the next thing" help you move forward in a situation you are struggling with right now?**

At the cross, we saw how Jesus cared for His mother by telling John to look after her. In the following passage, we see how Jesus cared for Mary Magdalene.

> **READ JOHN 20:1-2,11-18. What was Mary Magdalene's experience at the tomb? What did she think had happened to Jesus (vv. 1-2,11-15)?**

To Mary Magdalene, the worst had happened. Jesus was dead, and she didn't even know where His body was. She had come to the tomb with the other women to prepare His body for burial and perhaps to stay close to Jesus in her grief, but He was not there. As she wept, she heard someone speak to her. While it might sound harsh to us, the term "woman," was not a derogatory address in Jesus's day. Jesus also addressed His mother as "woman" on two occasions (John 2:4; 19:26).

> **What made Mary Magdalene recognize Jesus (v. 16)? Why do you think that made her realize it was Him?**

When someone uses our names, we feel known. In the early morning darkness, the grieving Mary hadn't recognized Jesus, but she knew Him when He said her name. I wonder if she recognized the tenderness and love in His voice.

I am reminded of the powerful words of Isaiah 43:1 that I often repeat to myself, "Fear not, for I have redeemed you; I have called you by name, you are mine . . . "

Jesus told Mary not to cling to Him or hold on to Him (v. 17). That may sound harsh, but Jesus wasn't rejecting Mary. He was going back to His Father soon, which meant He and Mary would have a new relationship—one where Jesus would never be apart from her again. She would soon have a different comfort and sense of His presence than she'd ever experienced before. Furthermore, Jesus charged her with the critical task of telling the disciples what had happened. Women's testimonies in that culture were usually dismissed, yet Jesus chose a woman whom He had delivered from a broken life, whom He saw, knew, and loved, to be the first person He appeared to and the one He commissioned to proclaim His resurrection.

Mary Magdalene constantly had her eyes on Jesus and didn't want to be apart from Him, even when the worst happened. How might the Lord be calling you to be more like Mary Magdalene?

DAY 2

The question we are wrestling with this week, *What if the worst happens?* arises from the fear that our nightmares will come true. It's comforting to me that people in the Bible struggled with the same fears I do, and that Scripture speaks to those fears.

(There are a lot of Scripture references today, so make use of the downloadable Scripture list PDF found at lifeway.com/desperateforhope.)

Let's take a look.

Fear: We or someone we love will face physical harm.

Biblical examples: The Israelites were afraid of their enemies (Num. 13:31); Elijah was afraid of Jezebel (1 Kings 19:3).

Truth to combat fear: God will fight for us (Ex. 14:14); the day of our death (and our loved ones' deaths) is determined by God (Ps. 139:16); worrying won't increase our lives (Matt. 6:27); God will never leave us (Matt. 28:20); even if suffering takes our lives, we will gain the crown of life (Rev. 2:10).

Fear: We will fail, feel ashamed, or look foolish.

Biblical examples: Gideon feared his family and later feared losing a battle (Judg. 6:27; 7:10); Jeremiah felt inadequate to speak well (Jer. 1:6).

Truth to combat fear: God will give us the words to speak (Jer. 1:7-8; Mark 13:11); God's wisdom is wiser than the world's (1 Cor. 1:25,27); God did not give us a spirit of fear (2 Tim. 1:7).

Fear: We will lose respect or power or experience rejection.

Biblical examples: Saul was afraid of David (1 Sam. 18:12); many were afraid to commit to Jesus due to social pressure (John 12:42-43).

Truth to combat fear: Since God is for us, we don't need to fear (Ps. 56:8-11; Rom. 8:31), especially because fearing people is a snare (Prov. 29:25). We can expect rejection and persecution (Matt. 5:11-12), but God will stand by us (2 Tim. 4:17) and will ensure nothing separates us from His love (Rom. 8:35-39).

Fear: We won't get what we've always longed for.

Biblical example: Rachel felt she needed children or life wasn't worth living (Gen. 30:1).

Truth to combat fear: God will supply the grace for everything He has called us to (2 Cor. 9:8). God will provide for our every need (Phil. 4:13), giving us everything necessary for life and godliness (2 Pet. 1:3).

Fear: Our nightmares will come true.

Biblical example: All that Job feared happened (Job 3:25).

Truth to combat fear: Most of our nightmares won't come true so we may be needlessly living in dread of the future (Matt. 6:25-34). But even if the worst happens, we can trust that God will be with us (Ps. 23:4).

Which of the listed fears can you relate to? Explain.
What other fears do you struggle with?

Look up the Scriptures listed in the previous section that speak to the fears that resonated with you. Was anything particularly encouraging? Was anything discouraging? Explain.

Our fears are often not related to what is immediately in front of us but rather what might happen in the future. We worry about receiving bad news, but God can deliver us even from that fear (Ps. 34:4).

READ PSALM 112:7-8a. Why did the psalmist say the righteous one is unafraid of bad news?

Looking back over what makes you afraid, consider for a moment what it would be like to face those situations without fear.

Read the following Scriptures, and write what you learn about facing difficult situations without fear.

- Deuteronomy 1:29-31

- 2 Chronicles 20:12

- Jeremiah 17:7-8

Scripture tells us that regardless of what we face, we can look to the Lord and put our trust in Him.

Read the following Scriptures and note whom you should fear and why.

- Psalm 25:12,14

- Psalm 111:10

- Matthew 10:28-31

The fear of the Lord—having a holy reverence for Him—delivers us from all other fears. After the disciples saw Jesus calm the tumultuous storm by His word, they were filled with holy fear, in awe that the wind and sea obeyed Him (Mark 4:41). They noted that His power was greater than what had frightened them. However, like the disciples, though we know that Jesus can rescue us from anything, we still struggle with fear. When we do, Psalm 56 offers comforting insight.

READ PSALM 56:3-4. **How would you summarize the truths found in this passage? How can you draw comfort from these verses?**

Fear encompasses a range of emotions, from unsettledness and anxiety to sheer terror. We tend to think that the opposite of being fearful is being fearless, unafraid, bold, and courageous in the face of danger. But the opposite of fear can also be serenity and peace in the face of uncertainty.

What do you most need when you are afraid? Courage or peace? Or both? Explain.

For years I had a sign on my desk, "Let your faith be greater than your fear," which reminded me to trust God when I was afraid. Sometimes that's easier said than done. On the next page are some ways I counter my own fears that may help you trust God when you're afraid.

1. Remember God's faithfulness. Reciting God's promises, His past faithfulness, and His character, will help us trust Him with our fears. The Israelites did that (Pss. 105; 107) and so did Jeremiah (Lam. 3:17-24).

2. Follow your fear and see where it takes you. Psalm 46 shows us that even if the world is falling apart, we don't have to be afraid. We can be still and know God's presence. For me, knowing I might eventually be a quadriplegic terrifies me. But when I'm able to verbalize my fear, I think of my friend Joni Eareckson Tada who has been a quadriplegic for decades and yet lives in joyful dependence on Jesus.

3. Trust that God will give you the grace that you need when you need it. God will give you all you need today, and He will do that tomorrow too (Matt. 6:34). Remember that God will supply all your needs (Phil. 4:19).

4. Remember that nothing comes into your life that has not passed through God's loving hands first. And if God has permitted it, He will use it both for your good and His glory (Rom. 8:28).

5. Remember that God is with you. He will never fail you or forsake you, and He will fight for you. No matter what you face, you won't walk through it alone (Deut 3:22; Heb. 13:5b-6).

6. Keep your mind and your thoughts on the Lord (Isa. 26:3, Rom. 8:6, Phil. 4:8-9).

7. Pray. Tell God your fears. Seek the Lord. Let Him know what you need and stay in constant conversation with Him (2 Chron. 20:3; Phil. 4:6-7).

Which of these actions stand out to you? Why? I encourage you to look up the related Scriptures and meditate on them.

When we ask, "What if the worst happens?" we can trust that God, who has already been to tomorrow, knows exactly what we'll need. It doesn't mean that the worst won't happen, because honestly our worst fears could materialize. No one is free from tragedy or pain, but no matter what happens, God will be there. He will be with you, and He will never leave you.

Several years ago I wrote an article entitled "What if the worst happens?"[2] In it, I talked about Shadrach, Meshach, and Abednego in Daniel 3, who were about to be thrown into the fire because they would not worship Nebuchadnezzar's gods or worship the golden statue he had erected. They said, "If we are thrown into the blazing furnace, the God we serve is able to deliver us from it . . . But even if he does not, we want you to know, Your Majesty, that we will not serve your gods . . ." (vv. 17-18, NIV).

Those three young men faced the fire without fear, trusting that God would be with them. They did not ask, "What if the worst happens?" but were satisfied knowing that even if the worst happened, God would take care of them. Replacing "what if" with "even if" is one of the most liberating exchanges we can ever make. We trade our irrational fears of an uncertain future for the loving assurance of an unchanging God. We see that even if the worst happens, God will carry us. He will still be good. He will never leave us. And He will supply all our needs. God's presence always comes with His provision; He will ensure we are taken care of.

READ PSALM 23. What does the Lord provide? Why was David not afraid of evil?

How have you experienced God's promise of presence and provision in the past? In what area of your life do you currently need to trust this promise?

Look over today's study. What has impacted you most? Ask the Lord how you need to apply what you've learned.

DAY 3

We looked closely at parts of John 20 on Day 1, understanding the passage in its context. Now as you listen to it being read, let the Holy Spirit speak to you through His Word another way.

> **Let's pray:**
>
> *Dear Lord, speak to me through Your Word and show me something of Yourself that I need to see. Help me to clear away all distractions and let Your Word, which is living and active, penetrate my heart, that I would encounter You.*

Use an audio Bible app or website to listen to John 20:1-2,11-18 being read aloud. (The YouVersion Bible app, Dwell Bible app, the her.bible website, and biblegateway.com are a few options.)

> **As you listen, put yourself in the scene. What phrases do you notice? What do you see? Write anything that speaks to you from hearing the passage.**

> **How has this Scripture affected your understanding of God's care in your losses and longings?**

> **How do you see Jesus differently from studying this story?**

My journal entry from November 6, 2009, read:

I feel so unloved . . . Just as Jacob wrestled with You and asked You for a blessing, I ask you to bless me, Lord. Honestly, after the polio clinic appointment, I feel I would be better off dead . . . Lord, what is Your invitation to me? I can't do it all. Everything is being stripped away. I have nothing and I cry out to you. I can't be strong. I can't wrestle with You. I can't do it anymore. Please. Turn something around. Make the pain stop. Help me to hear from You in our group today.

I was at one of the lowest points of my life. When I walked in to meet a group of friends, I started crying. Uncontrollably. My husband had left and was living with another woman. Both my daughters were angry, missing their dad and each trying to process what had happened. One was cagey about what she was doing, constantly out with friends. The other was angry and withdrawn, lashing out whenever she emerged from her room. Besides that, the air-conditioning at our house was broken, the toilet was leaking, and my car needed repairs. My body was getting weaker, and I'd fallen several times. I wondered how long my failing arms could keep making meals and driving the girls where they needed to go. Mostly I was afraid of the future. What would happen to the girls? And to me?

My friends sat with me in silence because no one knew exactly what to say. I appreciated the quiet because I couldn't handle trite answers or solutions. Finally, a friend spoke. She said,

"When I think of you and pray for you, I keep seeing this image. It's of the disciples and Jesus's mother Mary, weeping at the foot of the cross. They are huddled together, trying to comfort each other. Trying to make sense of what has happened. But it just doesn't make sense.

The sky is black, and all hope looks lost. Their dreams have died. It seems that nothing good will ever come from this. To them, this day, Good Friday, is the darkest day they've ever known.

But the one thing that they do not know is . . . Easter is coming."

Easter is coming. I could barely take in those words. But as the truth of them landed on me, I started crying again. Not tears of desperation but tears of hope. Easter was coming. The women at the cross had no idea what was going to happen. They could only see their pain in that moment. That's all I could see too.

As I sat with my friend's words, I realized my story wasn't over yet. God was not finished. There was so much I couldn't see. Her words gave me hope that God was already planting the seeds of good for me. He had not forgotten me. Perhaps Easter was just around the corner—the moment when everything would turn around. Or maybe I wouldn't experience the change until I entered heaven. Regardless of the timing, I realized that my suffering would not last forever.

Here's my journal entry from November 9, 2009, three days later:

> *I have a strange sense of peace from You in the midst of what seems like complete darkness. I am intrigued by the word* hope. *What does it really mean to have hope? Show me Lord . . . I cannot explain the joy and lightness of spirit You have given me. Only You could do this.*

Nothing in my circumstances had changed in those three days, but I was different. I had an underlying sense of hope.

Make a list of your current fears. What situations are keeping you up at night? In what areas of your life do you fear the worst will happen?

Write two possible outcomes to one of the fears from that list.

A. Write the best possible ending you can imagine where everything turns out as you want.

B. Write the worst possible ending where all your fears are realized.

We are all in the middle of our stories and can't see what's ahead. At the cross, it seemed as though the worst thing happened on Good Friday, but it turned out to be the best thing. We don't know God's timing in our lives; we may see our painful stories end well on earth or we may have to wait until heaven for our joyful ending.

As you consider outcome A, what do you need to pray for? Are you willing to pray for things you don't think God can do? Where do you need to believe that God can do the impossible? As Luke 1:37 says, "For nothing will be impossible with God."

As you consider outcome B, where is Jesus in this scenario? Does knowing He is with you help you as you think about the future? Is it possible to find hope and joy even in this possible ending? Explain.

The struggle we're dealing with today is often less debilitating than our fears about tomorrow. God will give us grace at the time to handle everything that He brings before us, but we cannot take hold of tomorrow's grace today. We must trust that it will be there.

How has today's study impacted you? Did it calm your fears or add to them? Explain. If you still feel unsettled, try to pinpoint why, and ask God to meet you in that fear.

DAY 4

My daughters have different fears than I do. Here is an excerpt from a Christmas letter about Kristi's fears as an adolescent:

> *Life with Kristi is an adventure. A few weeks ago, she ran into my room at 3 a.m., flipping on all the lights, screaming at the top of her lungs that there was an intruder in the house. Sitting bolt upright, about to dial 911, I asked where he was. She didn't know that; she only knew he left the toilet seat up. Suddenly she remembered a neighbor had used our bathroom that day . . .*

While I can tease Kristi about her fears, mine feel all too real. Fears based on my past experiences and wounds; events that other people can't fully understand.

The Lord understands our tendency to be anxious and afraid. As the psalmist said "For he knows what we are made of, remembering that we are dust" (Ps. 103:14, CSB). Being fearful is part of being human. In fact, the most frequent command in the Bible is to not fear or be afraid. Most Bible translations mention that command well over one hundred times. It's not a commandment meant to criticize and condemn but rather to comfort. God is calling us to find comfort in His presence in the midst of our fear.

When I'm afraid, I want to know that I'm not alone and that someone is going to help me. So I'm grateful that one of the most repeated promises in the Bible is that God is with us. It comes in the form of, "I will be with you" or "I am with you." But while we intellectually may know that God is always with us and that there is nowhere we can flee from His presence, believing that promise and experiencing His presence and comfort are different. How can we move from an academic knowledge that God is with us to a true assurance that He is? In some ways, it can be as simple as asking for an awareness of His presence and then paying attention to how He's answering. We can begin to sense God's nearness as we call on Him and seek His face, asking for signs of His loving presence as we move through our days. Perhaps that evidence could take the form of receiving unexpected wisdom after we've asked for it. Or feeling inexplicable peace after we've prayed. Or finding comfort and hope after we've read Scripture.

Pairing the most frequent command with the most repeated promise gives us the reason not to fear. No matter what happens, Jesus will be with us. He is our peace. Just as my daughter Kristi ran to my room in the middle of the night, we need to run to God when we are afraid. We do not know the future, but the Lord does. He has already been there. And He has given us all we need to face whatever will happen.

God promises to be with us, but because the things of this world are visible and more tangible than God, it's easy to trust and treasure them more than His presence. Throughout the Old Testament, the children of Israel sought God's gifts above God Himself, though Moses kept reminding them to worship and treasure God alone.

> **READ EXODUS 33:1-3.** What was God promising the Israelites through Moses? What was the one thing the Lord was not offering them?

> Would you want constant protection, clear direction, victory over your enemies, and all your needs abundantly provided for, but without the presence of God? Be honest and explain.

> **READ EXODUS 33:12-17.** How did Moses intercede for the people? What two things did God promise Moses in His response (v. 14)?

We are assured that in Christ, we will have both of those things (Matt. 11:28-30; Heb. 13:5-6). How does that give you peace?

Moses wanted God's presence more than His blessings (v. 15). Do you? If not, ask God to help you want His presence more than His presents.

With Jesus we'll always be safe, but that doesn't mean the worst won't happen. In fact, some of my nightmares came true. My son died. My husband abandoned our family. My body is failing. Yet God has unfailingly provided for me. And He will do the same for you. God has not only been good to me; He's been better than I imagined. When we're convinced that God is bigger than anything we'll face and that He'll always be with us, we can take hold of lasting peace. If that seems impossible right now, lean into God and let Him support you, asking Him to increase your faith (Luke 17:5) and to give you a sense of His presence. As you do, you'll find an other-worldly peace, as Jesus promised His disciples on the night before He was crucified.

READ JOHN 16:33. Where does Jesus tell us we will find peace?

What do we find in the world?

Why did Jesus say we should take heart or be courageous?

Do these words encourage you? Explain.

One of my go-to Scriptures when I am afraid is Isaiah 41:10. Write it below.

What two things does God tell us not to do? What five promises are those commands based on?

Years ago, I told a friend that I was terrified of what might happen in the future. She asked me to detail each fear, and for each one, she asked, "So where is Jesus in that fear?" I first answered vaguely, but she insisted I picture Jesus with me through everything that could go wrong. I needed to keep my eyes on Him. Every time we talked, she asked the same questions and soon I instinctively looked for Jesus whenever I felt afraid. It made the future feel less frightening.

Her words reminded me of a verse we looked at earlier, 2 Chronicles 20:12b, "For we are powerless against this great horde that is coming against us. We do not know what to do, but our eyes are on you."

After feeding five thousand people, Jesus insisted His disciples board a boat and go to the other side of the sea while He went alone to pray. Later, a violent storm erupted, buffeting their boat. In the middle of the storm, they saw Jesus walking on the water toward them. The disciples were terrified, but Jesus reassured them saying, "Have courage! It is I. Don't be afraid" (v. 27, CSB). Peter followed Jesus's words with the challenge: "Lord, if it's you . . . command me to come to you on the water" (v. 28, CSB).

What happened to Peter and why (vv. 29-30)?

Like Peter, when I'm looking directly at Jesus, I'm not overwhelmed by what's happening around me. But when I take my eyes off Him and focus on the storm I'm in, I give in to fear and sink.

What are the wind and the waves in your life today? How can you keep your eyes on Jesus?

What did Peter do as he started to sink?

Peter immediately called out to Jesus in his fear. After pulling Peter from the water, Jesus questioned Peter about his faith. Notice that Jesus didn't say Peter had no faith, just little faith. Inconsistent. Immature. Halting. But it was a faith that would grow as it was tested.[3] Our faith is much the same; it grows as we walk with Christ. The fierceness of the storms may not diminish, but our growing trust in the Savior helps us face them with less fear.

Have you ever experienced peace in a storm? Explain.

The account in Matthew 14 revealed to the disciples that Jesus is God. It also shows us that His presence brings peace. I tend to think of peace as the time after the storm blows over, when my struggles disappear, and everything is calm. Yet often the wind and waves don't get smaller but instead continue to grow. The peace of Jesus is not only finding rest after the storm, but in the middle of it.

Let's pray:

Dear Lord, You promise us peace, which is based on who You are and not our circumstances. When I am afraid, help me to put my trust in You. Remind me that You are always with me and help me to keep my eyes on You. Please give me an abiding and supernatural sense of peace this week.

I'm praying 2 Thessalonians 3:16 for you: "Now may the Lord of peace himself give you peace at all times in every way. The Lord be with you all."

DAY 5

We started this week asking the big question: *What if the worst happens?* Has this week's study helped answer that question? Explain.

How have you experienced God's love and faithfulness toward you this week? Where have you sensed His presence? Pay attention to signs of His love and presence through specific incidents like answers to prayer, unexpected peace, and comfort after reading Scripture.

How is God working in you? In your suffering?

READ ISAIAH 41:13. How does this verse reinforce truths from this lesson?

Do you sense that Jesus is in your situation with you right now? Explain.

What fears about the future are you holding on to?

Tim Keller says, "The peace of God is not the absence of fear. It, in fact, is His presence."[4] How does that statement tie into this lesson?

Read the following statements about peace. Choose one statement, look up the verse, write that verse on a sticky note or note card, and put it in a prominent place to help you take hold of God's peace.

When I'm focused on the Lord, He will give me perfect peace.
READ ISAIAH 26:3.

Even when the world is falling apart, God's love and peace surround me.
READ ISAIAH 54:10.

God gives me a supernatural peace that I cannot find apart from Him.
READ JOHN 14:27.

God's peace, which is beyond understanding, will help me trust Jesus and not be anxious.
READ PHILIPPIANS 4:7.

God can give me peace in every situation.
READ 2 THESSALONIANS 3:16.

Final Thought

We have eternal union with Christ when we come to Him in faith, receiving Him as Savior and Lord. We are assured that He will always be with us. But our daily communion with Him, the awareness of His presence and our fellowship with Him may not be constant. Fears, distractions, and sin can interrupt our fellowship with Him. We will find the richest communion when we lean on Him in dependence, seek His forgiveness, trust Him to provide, intentionally seek His face, and pay attention to His work in our lives. When we do so, our eyes are opened to see how God is providing for us. Psalm 77:19 reminded the Israelites and us that it's sometimes difficult to see what God is doing: "Your way was through the sea, your path through the great waters; yet your footprints were unseen." Ask the Lord to show you how He's providing.

Consider how you are trying to live independently from God by craving certainty rather than resting in His presence and provision. Do you believe that God alone is enough? Journal your thoughts about what the Lord shows you.

WHAT IF THE WORST HAPPENS?

Watch the Session 4 video and take notes below.

GROUP DISCUSSION / QUESTIONS FOR REFLECTION

What part of the video teaching was most significant for you? Why?

What are the things that keep you up at night? Your worst fears? What happens if you constantly focus on those things?

Vaneetha quoted Paul Tripp: "You never just suffer the thing that you're suffering, but you always also suffer the way that you're suffering that thing."[5] What does that mean and how has it been true for you?

How can you know God will be faithful even if the worst does happen?

How have you seen God provide exactly what you need when you need it?

How has your view of suffering been affected by what you've learned today?

What's one thing you've learned this week of study that better equips you to help others who are suffering?

To access the video teaching sessions, use the instructions in the back of your Bible study book.

Question

WHY IS GOD LETTING ME SUFFER?

DAY 1

I remember being fifteen years old, constantly wondering if people cared about me. I recall one Saturday in particular when I was hoping to talk to someone. However, my parents were feverishly cleaning the house, my sister was busy, and my friends all had plans. I felt slighted by everyone. When my dad asked me to run an errand with him, I grudgingly agreed. *No one cares about what I want,* I thought. But when I got home and opened the front door, a crowd jumped out and screamed "Surprise!" It was a party for my sixteenth birthday! It suddenly all made sense. While I thought everyone was ignoring me, they had actually been planning something wonderful for me.

I couldn't see beyond what was happening in the moment. Similarly, we know that God has great plans for us and everything He does is purposeful, but we may not see anything good as we struggle through our pain and loss. Yet amid our grief, God gives us the strength to endure. We know He is working for our eternal joy and His glory and that one day we will see how the pieces fit together. This is the second 3 Ps anchor that has sustained me in my suffering—knowing my pain has PURPOSE.

Last week we looked at two of the women at the cross: Mary, the mother of Jesus, and Mary Magdalene. We learned that keeping our eyes on Jesus, knowing that He is with us, is the best way to find peace in uncertainty and pain. This week, we'll see that God has purpose in our suffering as we study Naomi's story in the book of Ruth. Even after her crushing losses and belief that God was against her, she still didn't turn away from Him. As she kept doing what was in front of her, her suffering led to a greater redemption than she could have imagined.

Before we dive into the details, let's get an overview of the story.

READ RUTH 1. Jot down your initial observations. Where do you see hints of God's favor toward Naomi? What resonates with you?

Now let's take a closer look.

REREAD RUTH 1:1-5. When did this story take place?

READ JUDGES 2:17-19 AND 21:25. What characterized Israel's conditions during that time?

List the suffering this family experienced.

Each tragedy Naomi suffered represents a layered loss. Consider and note the various difficulties Naomi might have experienced with each loss. I've completed the first as an example.

FAMINE. DECISION TO LEAVE BETHLEHEM.	Fear of starvation. Leaving family and friends for Moab. Fear of the unknown. Wondering if this was the right decision.
LIVING IN A FOREIGN COUNTRY WITH A DIFFERENT LANGUAGE AND RELIGION.	

THE DEATH OF HER HUSBAND, LEAVING HER ALONE WITH TWO SONS.	
DAUGHTERS-IN-LAW WITH AN UNFAMILIAR CULTURAL AND RELIGIOUS BACKGROUND.	
THE DEATH OF BOTH SONS, LEAVING HER WITH NO GRANDCHILDREN AND NO BLOOD RELATIVES IN MOAB.	

Can you relate to any of Naomi's experiences or the emotions she might have felt? Explain.

Here is a brief history of Moab: Abraham's nephew, Lot, had two daughters whose fiancés died. Desperate to preserve Lot's bloodline, the oldest got her father drunk and slept with him (unbeknownst to him) because she wanted a child. Definitely an R-rated dysfunctional family story! Her son was the father of the Moabite nation, which was constantly at odds with Israel. The Moabite king hired Balaam to curse Israel, and as a result, God forbade Moabites to enter the assembly of the Lord, even to the tenth generation (Deut. 23:3-5).

Naomi knew the Lord and referred to Him as Yahweh (written in your Bible as "LORD"), which is Israel's covenant name for God. She most likely knew the warnings about Moab in Scripture. So perhaps Naomi wondered whether these tragedies were her fault for moving to Moab and letting her sons marry Moabite women.

Scripture doesn't give us a reason for Naomi's tragedies, but it does tell us that God redeemed Naomi's circumstances, making her part of the bloodline of Christ.

How does that encourage you?

Scripture is clear that suffering is often unrelated to sin. The righteous suffer at times, as we see in the life of Job. Psalm 103:10 says, "He does not deal with us according to our sins, nor repay us according to our iniquities."

Have you ever felt that your suffering was a punishment from God? If so, what were the circumstances? How do the following verses address that issue?

- Isaiah 53:4-5

- Romans 8:1

- Romans 8:32

- 2 Corinthians 5:21

While death and suffering are a result of the fall (Rom. 5:12), suffering is never a condemnation or punishment from God for the Christian. Christ bore the penalty of our sin on the cross. God is FOR you.

However, God's favor doesn't mean that our suffering is never related to our actions. Sometimes we experience natural consequences for our sin; if we steal, we could go to jail. Additionally, God may use our suffering to discipline and teach us, but it is always for our good. To further understand godly discipline, read Hebrews 12:5-11. For those who don't know Jesus, suffering is always an invitation to turn to Him.

> READ RUTH 1:6-14. What did Naomi decide to do and why? How did that decision and her words to Orpah and Ruth show her courage and endurance?

> What did Naomi ask of or say about the Lord in verses 6, 8, 9, 13?

> READ RUTH 1:15-18. What did Naomi urge Ruth to do?

> How did Ruth respond to Naomi? What name for God did Ruth use in verse 17? What does that show you about Naomi? About Ruth?

The first mention in the book of Ruth of other gods besides the LORD is in verses 15-18. The Moabites' god was Chemosh, who approved of human sacrifice (2 Kings 3:26-27). Perhaps Ruth was drawn to God because of Naomi's relationship with Him. Naomi seemed to see the hand of God in everything—and trusted Him enough to complain bitterly.

Naomi was uncomfortably honest about how she felt. How are Naomi's words and attitude similar to the laments we studied last week?

You may be surprised by Naomi's honest assessment that God was against her. Yet despite all that had happened, she still believed in God, believed He was sovereign over all that happened, and was willing to entrust herself to Him. She journeyed to Bethlehem, acknowledging she'd been dealt a bitter hand, perhaps believing her path would remain rocky. But she still moved toward God and His people.

What from Naomi's story and attitude can you apply to your own life? Sit with all you've learned today and write any insights.

DAY 2

In the ancient world, names often described a person's character. Naomi's name meant *pleasant*, but when she returned to Bethlehem, she asked to be called *Mara* which means *bitter.*

> Why did Naomi want her name changed? What does her given name imply about her character?

> Have circumstances changed the way you view yourself and your life? What name would you choose to describe your outlook in this season of life?

> Do you think Naomi was viewing God correctly in Ruth 1:20-21? Why or why not?

> Does God ever afflict His people? Use these passages to help you answer: Job 1:12; Psalm 119:71,75.

What truths was Naomi possibly not considering? Use these passages to help you answer: Psalm 145:17; Isaiah 30:18-21; Jeremiah 31:3; Lamentations 3:32-33.

We see that God does afflict His people at times, but that affliction is never outside His character and purpose. He uses all the circumstances of our lives— even the bitter ones—for our good, though we often cannot see it at the time.

Can you relate to Naomi's words in verses 20-21? Explain.

READ RUTH 2:1-3.

Chapter 2 begins with the narrator setting the stage for Boaz to enter the story. We learn that Boaz is related to Elimelech, Naomi's late husband, which is key in the unfolding story.

What did Ruth request and how does it highlight her character?

Ruth took it upon herself to provide for Naomi, asking permission to gather grain. God provided for foreigners, the poor, and widows through gleaning, which is gathering grain left in the field after the harvest. In Leviticus 19:9-10 and Deuteronomy 24:19, God commanded the Israelites not to reap to the very edges of their fields or gather the gleaning of the harvest so that those in need could have grain to pick up.

According to the narrator, how did Ruth end up in Boaz's field (v. 3)? Where do you think God was in this situation? Does Proverbs 16:9 add to your understanding?

We'll be skipping much of the narrative in this study, so if you have time, read the rest of Ruth; it's a beautiful love story. Ruth worked hard in the field and found favor with the owner, Boaz, who was a righteous man. She reported his kindness back to Naomi.

READ RUTH 2:19-20 BELOW:

And her mother-in-law said to her, "Where did you glean today? And where have you worked? Blessed be the man who took notice of you." So she told her mother-in-law with whom she had worked and said, "The man's name with whom I worked today is Boaz." And Naomi said to her daughter-in-law, "May he be blessed by the LORD, whose kindness has not forsaken the living or the dead!" Naomi also said to her, "The man is a close relative of ours, one of our redeemers."

Contrast Naomi's words about God here with those in Ruth 1:13,20-21. What do you notice?

When Ruth told Naomi about Boaz, Naomi remembered that Boaz was a close relative. Judging from her words in Ruth 1:11-13, Naomi had seemingly forgotten about that connection. It's easy to assume, as Naomi did, that our situation is hopeless and not see how God may be providing for us.

Think about the struggles you are currently facing. Can you see any signs of God's kindness? If not, ask Him to reveal even a flicker of light now or over the next few days.

After Naomi learned about Boaz's favor toward Ruth, she devised a plan for Boaz to redeem Ruth. The law allowed close relatives to marry childless widows to perpetuate their family name and inheritance, which Boaz ultimately did.

READ RUTH 4:13-17. How had Naomi's present and future turned around? Who was behind that?

How did the neighborhood women celebrate how Naomi's life had changed from what she said about herself in Ruth 1:21? How does Matthew 1:5, which is part of the genealogy of Christ, add to your understanding?

God had a greater purpose behind Naomi's tragedies than she could have seen. Her grandson was in the line of Christ. Naomi was part of the greatest redemption story.

Our stories are folded into the grand story that God is writing, which is about His glory and goodness to us. Like Naomi, we will always carry our past losses with us, but we can trust that God has purpose in everything. We see our present and what's around us, while God knows our tomorrow. And He's preparing us for our future through what's happening today.

After the initial tragedies that opened the story, we see signs of God's kindness and redemption toward Naomi breaking through, even after Naomi felt that the Lord was against her.

Think about the passages you've read over the last two days and list the glimpses of God's kindness to Naomi you've noticed.

After you've finished your list, read the following and circle what you hadn't noticed.

God broke the famine, visited His people, and gave them food (Ruth 1:6).

God provided a daughter-in-law, Ruth, who chose to follow God and pledged to stay with her (1:16).

God brought them back to Bethlehem at the beginning of barley harvest (1:22).

God provided a way for widows and foreigners to gather food at harvest time (Lev. 19:9-10).

God brought Ruth to Boaz's field (2:3), and God ensured Boaz noticed her faithfulness (2:11-12).

God provided Boaz for Ruth—a worthy, generous, older man from Elimelech's clan to be a kinsman redeemer (2:1,10,14-17,20)

God enabled Ruth to conceive though she hadn't had a child with Mahlon (4:10,13).

God did not leave Naomi or us without a Redeemer (4:15)

What have you learned from Naomi's experience that you can apply to your own?

Naomi never turned from God in her suffering, even when she felt He was against her. She kept persevering, moving forward, recognizing God's hand in her life, and being open to Him. The Lord changed her through that process.

READ ROMANS 5:3-5. Where do you see evidence of those characteristics in Naomi? Where do you see them in your life?

What have you learned about God and His purposes through today's study? How does what you've learned answer the question "Why is God letting me suffer?" What aspects of God found in Naomi's story do you need to lean on in your current situation?

Naomi's story of endurance and redemption may help you see that even when God feels far away—when you think He has turned against you and you see nothing good ahead—He is working for a greater good than you can imagine. He is sovereign over all that happens, working through your sins and mistakes, and through your bitter providences to bring you unimaginable good and glory. Your suffering has purpose. You may get a glimpse of what He's doing in this life, as Naomi did, but you will see it more clearly in heaven.

DAY 3

We've looked closely at Ruth 1, understanding the passage within its context. Now let's listen to it being read and let the Holy Spirit speak to you through His Word another way.

Let's pray:

Dear Lord, speak to me through Your Word and show me something of Yourself that I need to see. Help me to clear away all distractions and let Your Word, which is living and active, penetrate my heart, so that I would encounter You.

Use an audio Bible app or website to listen to Ruth 1 being read aloud. (The YouVersion Bible app, Dwell Bible app, the her.bible website, and biblegateway.com are a few options.)

As you listen, put yourself in the scene. What phrases do you notice? What do you see? Write anything that speaks to you from hearing the passage.

How has this Scripture affected your understanding of loss and longings?

How do you see the Lord differently from studying this story?

I contracted a mild case of polio as an infant in India, but the doctor's misdiagnosis left me completely paralyzed. Because some muscles inexplicably regenerated later, combined with twenty-one surgeries, I was eventually able to live a normal life, albeit with significant limitations. I went out-of-state to college, lived and worked in Boston, moved across the country to business school, got married, had a busy career, and then had children. As a young mom, I was obsessed with all things creative like cooking, scrapbooking, painting, and making jewelry. I pushed myself past my limits.

Then the escalating pain and weakness started. After countless medical appointments, I was eventually diagnosed with post-polio syndrome, a debilitating condition that would likely leave me a quadriplegic again. The doctors were adamant that I immediately stop doing everything nonessential, saying the more I did, the weaker I would get. They likened my energy to money in a bank—everything I did was making a withdrawal. My job was to conserve my strength.

I was devastated. I couldn't see how God could possibly use this horrifying diagnosis, and I wondered how I could endure it. I had so many questions—Why would God make me creative, let me love cooking and painting, have two young daughters to take care of, and then take all my strength away? Why would God do this to me after I'd been faithful?

In my journal dated May 2, 2003, several weeks after my diagnosis, I wrote:

> *I feel trapped inside my body. I go back and forth between depression and hope because You have ordained this. I would never have chosen this path and feel injustice and regret over what is happening, but I give it to You. Use it for Your glory and help me to see it as beautiful . . . I asked You to help me put to death pride in my life—continual dependence will do that. But does it have to be this way?*

> *I need to trust that You are sufficient and may call me to depend on others. But I don't want others to have power over me. To say no and leave me alone and vulnerable. I remember being in the hospital—being helpless and unable to do anything for myself. Waiting for someone to bring me a bedpan to go to the*

bathroom. I never wanted to live my life that way again. The hardest thing about this is the loss of my self-sufficiency. But I see You asking me, "How much do you want of Me?" It's been a hard ten years and each loss has been so hard but with what You've taken away, I see You so much more clearly.

Lord, help me to worship where I am—not where I want to be.

This quote from A Grief Observed *is staying with me. "The more we believe that God hurts only to heal—the less we can believe that there is any use in begging tenderness. A cruel man might be bribed . . . but suppose that what you are up against is a surgeon whose intentions are wholly good. The kinder and more conscientious he is, the more inexorably he will go on cutting. If he yielded to your entreaties—if he stopped before the operation was complete—all the pain up to that point would have been useless."[1]*

I gave up my hobbies as my body got weaker. I started writing using voice recognition software just to process my thoughts since typing was no longer an option. Years later, after my husband left, I started blogging, and a major Christian website providentially ran an article that I submitted to them. The enthusiastic response from readers surprised me. I never thought God would give me a ministry through writing.

While I still grieve what I've lost and continue to lose, God has used those losses in unanticipated ways. Writing has become what painting used to be—a way to express my creativity, with the added joy of knowing that my words are helping others. Seeing my pain accomplish a greater purpose has helped me process that ongoing loss.

Suffering can blur your perspective, especially if you view it through the lens of despair. It's easy to assume your present pain will go on forever, that God is against you, or that your entire life is a mess. Those are lies from Satan, which can make you feel trapped, convinced the situation cannot change. To pull out of it, you need to reframe your perspective.

Your struggles are not a punishment for your past but can be a preparation for your future. Your story is enfolded in God's story; He is in sovereign control of your life. Reframing the narrative of your suffering to see God's role in it and remembering your pain will end and does not define you, can transform how you experience it.

For the exercise below, choose a current difficult situation you're walking through and view it through different lenses. I'll give you an example to help clarify this after I explain the exercise.[2]

As you consider your situation through the first lens, the lens of despair, imagine it is:

- Personal: It's ALL your fault; God is against you.

- Pervasive: The problem is widespread and extends to your whole life.

- Permanent: It will never end.

As you look at your situation through the second lens, the lens of truth, view it as:

- Not personal: It's not ALL your fault, and God is for you.

- Specific: It's limited to this situation.

- Temporary: This will end and will one day be redeemed.

In terms of fault and responsibility, take everything before the Lord and ask Him to reveal what you need to see, need to repent of, or need help to change.

Read the following example before you begin.
Situation: You have a rebellious and destructive teenager.

LENS OF DESPAIR

- Personal: This is completely my fault. I'm an awful parent. God is against me and is punishing me.

- Pervasive: I'm not just a horrible mother to my children; I'm also a bad friend and wife. Nothing is going right. God is taking everything away to make me miserable.

- Permanent: This will never change. My child will end up in jail, and nothing good will ever happen. God will not help me or my child because God can't change this.

LENS OF TRUTH

- Not personal: My child is responsible for himself and is making his own choices. This doesn't mean I'm a bad parent, though I will ask God to show me my responsibility. God is for me, and He is not punishing me.

- Specific: This struggle is specific to this child and his situation. God gives and takes away for my good and His glory. I can find joy in other places.

- Temporary: This rebellion may just be temporary, and my child may learn about God through this. Regardless, God is using the situation, can change it instantly, will give me endurance as I wait, and will one day redeem it.

Summarize YOUR difficult situation:

What would you tell yourself if you viewed your difficult situation through the lens of despair?

- ◆ Personal:

- ◆ Pervasive:

- ◆ Permanent:

What would you tell yourself if you viewed your situation as part of God's bigger story through the lens of truth?

- ◆ Not personal:

- ◆ Specific:

- ◆ Temporary:

As you reflect on your current situation, write something positive that has come from this trial that could be part of God's purpose. Consider how your struggle has impacted your relationship with Him, your witness, and your character.

DAY 4

Things rarely turn out as I expected or planned. Years ago, we took a family trip to India, hoping that it would be an unforgettable and educational trip for the girls. Here is an excerpt from our 2007 Christmas letter:

> *The trip was incredible: the Taj Mahal, a jungle safari, the spice market in Old Delhi, an exotic animal zoo, ancient monuments, the opulent palace at Mysore, along with family gatherings. But it turned out that the girls' favorite part of the trip wasn't the Taj Mahal, the safari, seeing family, or even the zoo, but rather "the snacks on the bus to Agra" followed closely by "the hotel swimming pool."*

While the things I've planned often go awry, I'm thankful that God's plans never do.

I came to Christ after reading about Jesus healing the blind man in John 9. I'd been asking God why I'd gotten polio while other people's lives looked so easy. I wondered what I'd done to deserve so much pain. The disciples asked related questions—and God answered them, and me, through the following passage:

READ JOHN 9:1-3. What did the disciples' question reveal about their views on suffering?

What's your first reaction to Jesus's response?

The disciples' question was related to the cause of suffering, but Jesus's answer was related to the purpose. How can that be a helpful distinction?

Jesus healed the blind man (John 9:7) who later became a follower of Christ (John 9:35-38). Though I came to Christ through this passage, I didn't think that all suffering had a purpose—there was too much pain and evil in the world to believe that. It took many years before I was convinced of God's sovereignty over everything.

I want to give you some insight into my journey to understand God's sovereignty by sharing quotes from Scripture, books, and sermons and how they influenced me along the way. Each segment is followed by a list of several Scriptures. Choose one or two to read, then write your reflection about what you learn from the passages and how they relate to the quote or paragraph above it.

1. GOD DOESN'T MAKE MISTAKES.

In early 1996, a friend quoted a paraphrase of Psalm 119:68a saying, "God is good, and everything He does is good." I thought about those words for days.

LOOK UP PSALM 119:68A and write it below.

Soon afterward, I started teaching a study for my church on Evelyn Christensen's book, *What Happens When Women Pray*. When I came to the chapter entitled "God Never Makes a Mistake," I assumed the author hadn't suffered. But then I learned she'd had three miscarriages, a stillborn baby, and an infant who died at seven months old. I spent hours reading the Bible, trying to figure out if her words were true.

She'd written:

> *This is the place you reach when after years and years of trials and difficulties you see that all has been working out for your good, and that God's will is perfect. You see that He has made no mistakes. He knew all of the "what ifs" in your life. When you finally recognize this, even during your trials, it's possible to have joy, deep down joy.*[3]

Almost a year later, when my son died, I spoke at his funeral saying, "God never makes a mistake," greatly comforted by those words.

SCRIPTURE: Numbers 23:19; Deuteronomy 32:4; Psalm 18:30

YOUR REFLECTION:

2. GOD IS SOVEREIGN OVER MY SUFFERING.

While I believed that God never makes a mistake when I spoke at my son Paul's funeral, I struggled to accept it later. Months afterward, I heard about Charles Spurgeon, a faithful British preacher in the 1800s who struggled with lifelong, debilitating depression and died of gout and kidney disease at age 57. When asked how he felt about his situation, he responded:

> *It would be a very sharp and trying experience to me to think that I have an affliction which God never sent me—that the bitter cup was never filled by His hand, that my trials were never measured out by Him, nor sent to me by His arrangement of their weight and quantity.*[4]

This quote stunned me. Spurgeon was sure that all his struggles were sent specifically and directly by God. Realizing that God had carefully weighed my trials, nothing in my life was arbitrary, and that God had put boundaries on my suffering was a huge comfort.

SCRIPTURE: Isaiah 45:6-7; Lamentations 3:32-33; Matthew 10:29; Acts 17:26-27; Romans 8:28-29

YOUR REFLECTION:

3. GOD'S PLAN CANNOT BE STOPPED.

As I was puzzling out these radical ideas, I picked up Joni Eareckson Tada's book *When God Weeps*. I was unprepared for how deeply it would change me. Joni says:

> *Nothing happens by accident . . . not even tragedy . . . not even sins committed against us . . . Every sorrow we taste will one day prove to be the best possible thing that could have happened. We will thank God endlessly in heaven for the trials He sent us here . . .* [5]

> *Either God rules, or Satan sets the world's agenda and God is limited to reacting. In which case, the Almighty is Satan's clean-up boy . . . finding a way to wring good out of the situation somehow. But it wasn't His best for you, wasn't Plan A, wasn't exactly what He had in mind. In other words, although God would manage to patch things up, your suffering itself would be meaningless.* [6]

Satan does have a part in our suffering, but he cannot harm us in ways that God doesn't permit. If he could, that would make God Satan's clean-up boy and would render our suffering meaningless. But our suffering isn't meaningless, and Satan has limited power. God's plan cannot be thwarted by mistakes, sinful actions, or Satan's schemes.

SCRIPTURE: Genesis 50:20; Job 1:6-12; Isaiah 43:13; Lamentations 3:37-38; Luke 4:1-2; 1 Peter 5:8-10

YOUR REFLECTION:

4. GOD'S WAYS ARE NOT MY WAYS.

To believe that God had good purposes in my suffering, I needed to see that He was loving and wise as well as in complete control. We cannot trust a God who loves us and weeps with us but cannot help us. If God can't help us, we have no guarantee that any of His promises will come true. Yet we are still left with the question of why all this happened. Why does God permit suffering? What good will it do?

The short answer is that God's ways are a mystery. In this life we may not understand what God is doing, but we can trust He has a purpose.

SCRIPTURE: Isaiah 55:8-9; John 13:4-7; 1 Corinthians 2:9-10; 1 Corinthians 13:12

YOUR REFLECTION:

5. GOD HAS A PURPOSE.

Although we cannot see all of God's purposes, we may see a few. John Piper said:

God is always doing 10,000 things in your life, and you may be aware of three of them . . . Not only may you see a tiny fraction of what God is doing in your life; the part you do see may make no sense to you.[7]

Suffering often feels senseless. It is hard to reconcile how we are protected by the power of God and yet endure fiery trials. But we can take comfort that our trials will not last forever and that God has a purpose in them.

SCRIPTURE: Isaiah 46:10; 1 Peter 1:5; 4:12; 5:10

YOUR REFLECTION:

Our suffering is always producing something, which James sees as a reason to rejoice.

READ JAMES 1:2-4. According to this passage, how are we to view trials? Does that seem realistic to you? Explain.

Why do trials test our faith? Has that been your experience? Explain.

Trials have tested my faith as I've wondered why God allowed them, how long they'd last, and how things would turn out.

List everything trials produce. How do we let endurance have its full effect?

It's encouraging that hard-won endurance from going through trials matures our faith and gives us strength to withstand future trials. But to realize its full effect, we shouldn't fight against the process. We need to lean into God, trusting that He's using every drop of our heartache for our ultimate good.

Trials usually begin with a lack or loss, but James says their result is that we'd lack nothing. How is that possible?

It seems unrealistic that we could lack nothing in the midst of a crisis when there are countless things we don't have. But by saying we lack nothing, we are declaring that God will provide everything we need and will use all we face to shape our character to be more like Jesus. For years I had a quote pinned to my bulletin board from John Newton: "Everything which he sends is needful; nothing can be needful which he withholds."[8] When we view all our circumstances through the lens of God's sovereign provision, we can truly live a life without lack.

Bonus Study

Read through the following list of some of God's purposes in suffering.

* Produces endurance, character, and hope (Rom. 5:3-5)

* Enables us to comfort others (2 Cor. 1:3-4)

* Teaches us to rely on Christ (2 Cor. 1:8-9)

* Makes us long for heaven, our true home (2 Cor. 4:16–5:5)

* Prepares us for a great reward (2 Cor. 4:17)

* Helps us know God better (Phil. 3:10)

* Refines our faith (1 Pet. 1:6-7)

Which of these have you experienced? When?

Look up the Scriptures in the list above and circle those that are most meaningful to you. How do they encourage you in what you're going through today?

DAY 5

We started this week asking the big question: *Why is God letting me suffer?* Has this week's study helped answer that question? Explain.

How have you experienced God's love and faithfulness toward you this week? Where have you sensed His presence? Pay attention to signs of His love and presence through specific incidents like answers to prayer, unexpected peace, and comfort after reading Scripture.

How is God working in you? In your suffering? Where have you seen hints of His purpose?

READ PSALM 71:19-21 AND JEREMIAH 29:11. How do these verses reinforce truths from this lesson?

Do you believe that the Lord only wants good for you? If not, why not? What's causing your struggle to believe? Explain.

Where specifically do you need to trust that God has a purpose—a "why" for what you're going through—even when you don't understand?

Paul David Tripp says: "The Bible teaches there is no situation, relationship, or circumstance that our Heavenly Father does not control. He has carefully administrated every detail in the story of our lives."[9]

How does that statement tie into this lesson? Do you agree with it? Why or why not?

Read the following statements about God's purpose and promises. Choose the statement that most resonates with you, look up the verse, write it on a note card, and put it in a prominent place to help you believe God has great plans for you.

Though people might try to harm me, God has planned everything for my good.
READ GENESIS 50:20.

God can do anything, and His plans can't be thwarted.
READ JOB 42:2.

God's ways are perfect, and His word proves true.
READ PSALM 18:30.

Even though we make plans, only God's purposes will come to pass.
READ PROVERBS 19:21.

Everything in our lives as Christians will work for our good.
READ ROMANS 8:28.

In the Introduction (page 6) and Session 2 (page 30), I asked you to make lists of the past negative events and low points of your life as well as the positive events and high points. You can fill those out on page 186 if you've not completed them yet or if you'd like to add to them. We will use those lists in the closing week.

Final Thought

We've seen how God showed Naomi kindness all along her path, even when she was convinced that God was against her. The wonderful and redemptive ending doesn't diminish her pain, but it does put her story in a different perspective, knowing God used it for her ultimate joy. Her trials had a purpose. All our experiences fit into His grand story to reconcile the world through Christ so we can delight in Him forever.

Drawing from the lists mentioned above, where have you seen God's kindness along the path you've been traveling? Do you see God's provision? Have you developed endurance? How has your suffering drawn you closer to Christ? Journal your thoughts.

SESSION 5: VIDEO VIEWER GUIDE

WHY IS GOD LETTING ME SUFFER?

Watch the Session 5 video and take notes below.

GROUP DISCUSSION / QUESTIONS FOR REFLECTION

What part of the video teaching was most significant for you? Why?

Does knowing God has purpose in your suffering help you endure the difficult times? Explain.

Vaneetha referenced the John Newton quote: "Everything which he sends is needful; nothing can be needful which he withholds." Do you agree with this statement? Is it comforting to you? Why or why not?

How have you seen God make something beautiful out of your heartache or the heartache of someone else?

How has your suffering changed you? Strengthened you? What have you learned in it?

How has your view of suffering been affected by what you've learned today?

What's one thing you've learned this week of study that better equips you to help others who are suffering?

To access the video teaching sessions, use the instructions in the back of your Bible study book.

Question

HOW CAN GOD USE MY SUFFERING WHEN I FEEL USELESS?

DAY 1

When I lived in Boston, I made plans to do something every night, mostly out of insecurity. I paid little attention to what my roommate was doing until one night when I asked her if she'd had a fun evening. She hesitated and said with tear-filled eyes, "No, it wasn't fun. I went to a movie alone because I didn't have anyone else to go with. I didn't ask you because you're always busy."

Her words took me aback. I'd been so wrapped up in my world that I hadn't noticed what or how she was doing. She went on to share how she'd been struggling with loneliness for a while. I marveled at her honesty, especially after I'd been so thoughtless. Our relationship quickly grew deeper, mostly because she was brave enough to tell me how I'd hurt her.

I now consider her one of my closest friends from my years in Boston. This showed me the power and impact of vulnerably reaching out even when we feel slighted.

The study from both this week and last week are grounded in the 3 Ps anchor of *PURPOSE*. In God's mysterious plan, He uses our suffering for our good and His glory. Last week we talked about how God uses our suffering for our eternal joy, for something bigger than we can see, even when all we see is loss. This week we'll see how God is glorified by what we experience. Today, we're studying the story of the Samaritan woman, which offers a beautiful picture of how one person's testimony of encountering Jesus in her brokenness can glorify God and transform an entire community. We'll see how God uses others to encourage us in our suffering and how we in turn can encourage them.

Before we dive into the details, let's get an overview of the story. As you read, pay attention to the power of the Samaritan woman's testimony.

READ JOHN 4:1-30,39-42. What do you notice? Is there anything surprising to you?

Let's start with a little background about Samaria. After King Solomon died in 931 BC, his kingdom (which was made up of the twelve tribes of Israel) split. The ten northern tribes became known as Israel and the two southern ones as Judah. The Assyrians destroyed Israel around 722 BC and deported most of the inhabitants of the land back to Assyria.[1] The Assyrians then populated Israel with a variety of pagan people. These new residents intermarried with the Jews who were left in the country, thus forming a mixed-race people. Their religion was a combination of pagan cultures mixed with the Jewish faith, and they settled in a region known as Samaria. Samaria lay directly between Judea and Galilee.

The Jews hated the Samaritans because they had corrupted the bloodline and the faith. Their animosity was so strong that often Jews would go around Samaria when traveling from Judea to Galilee rather than going through it. The Pharisees even called Jesus a Samaritan as an insult (John 8:48).

REREAD JOHN 4:1-15.

Here's some information to help set the context. Verse 6 says that Jesus sat down at the well at noon (or "sixth hour"), which was one of the hottest times of the day. Women usually went in the cool of morning or the evening to the well (Gen. 24:10-11) where they likely congregated and caught up with each other. Furthermore, it was culturally taboo for a Jewish man to speak to a woman alone, especially a Samaritan woman (vv. 9,27).

What were Jesus's first words to the Samaritan woman? Why might Jesus have initiated the conversation in this way?

What did Jesus offer the Samaritan woman, and how did she misunderstand the offer (vv. 10-15)?

REREAD JOHN 4:16-18. What do we learn about this woman's past? What is your initial reaction to this information? Explain.

Many regard her as a serial adulteress. But since women could not initiate divorce and the Jewish penalty for adultery was stoning (John 8:4-5), it's highly unlikely that she was.

We don't know why she had five husbands, why she was not married to the man she was living with, or why she came to the well at midday. Her story is likely layered with suffering, sin, and shame—as all our stories are. Perhaps her husbands were unfaithful, grew tired of her, or died in her arms. Perhaps through childhood trauma and adult wounds, she believed she was not enough and the multiple men she knew added to that narrative. Perhaps living with a man not her husband was her only means of support. Whatever the reason for her failed relationships, she likely carried the burden of shame and invisible scars to the well that day.

Has this information changed your opinion about the woman at the well? Explain.

Jesus knew her entire past. How would that have been life-giving for the Samaritan woman? How would it have been difficult?

REREAD JOHN 4:19-26. What did Jesus tell the Samaritan woman about His identity? Is this surprising to you? Why or why not?

This was Jesus's longest recorded private conversation with anyone in the Gospels, His first declaration that He was Messiah, and the only time He revealed His identity to a Gentile.

As you consider what Jesus did and said to the Samaritan woman, how did He make her feel seen, known, and loved? How did He encourage her and give her dignity?

The honor Jesus showed women throughout the Gospels is astonishing. In Session 1, Jesus met His beloved friends Mary and Martha with tears and truth. In Session 3, Jesus entrusted Mary Magdalene with the stunning news of His resurrection. And this session we discover that Jesus chose to first reveal His identity as Messiah to a Samaritan woman.

READ JOHN 4:27-30,39-42. How do verses 28-30 reveal life change in this woman? What was her testimony, and how is it an example for us in our own evangelism efforts?

How did the people respond (vv. 30,39)? What does that tell you about the woman's influence? Given that she'd been alone at the well, is this surprising to you? Why or why not?

Jesus offered the Samaritan woman living water, which she first misinterpreted. She was happy to sign up if it kept her from having to draw water from the well anymore, perhaps making it easier to elude people in her community. Yet the living water she ultimately received from Jesus brought her back into community. After her encounter with the Messiah, she left her water jar and ran back into town to tell her story to all the people she had worked so hard to avoid.

Why did people ultimately believe in Jesus (vv. 40-42)? How does that encourage you as you share your story?

It's easy to pull away from community in suffering, putting up walls of self-protection. Yet after the Samaritan woman met Jesus, she moved toward her community. Many from the town believed as a result of her testimony, without seeing healings or other miracles or even hearing a stirring sermon. It began with one woman's testimony. Given her struggles, she probably didn't realize the weight of her influence or the power of her witness. Perhaps you don't either.

Has Jesus met you in your suffering? Explain.

If not, stop and ask the Spirit to reveal His presence and love to you now. Ask for living water. READ EPHESIANS 3:14-19 and ask God to give you the power to understand His love.

If He has met you in your suffering, how can your story point to the power of the gospel and be a blessing to others? List a few people you can share your story with this week, along with some bullet points of what you might say.

Where can you relate to the Samaritan woman? What is Jesus offering you? Sit with all you've learned today, and write what the Lord might be showing you about your need, Jesus's care, and the importance of your story.

We may not think the body of Christ needs us when we are wounded, but our story of God's faithfulness amid shattered dreams may be the greatest witness we could ever offer. The world needs to see if our faith in God makes a difference in suffering. Are you willing to let God use you in this way?

DAY 2

God was glorified through the Samaritan woman's life, which was previously marked by suffering and shame. If you are struggling, you may wonder how God could use your life, especially if you feel like a burden to others. While I understand those feelings, when we as Christians turn to God in our suffering, it draws others to the Lord. Our suffering has a greater purpose than we can see or know. The Thessalonians are a great example of this truth.

OUR SUFFERING CAN BE A WITNESS

READ 1 THESSALONIANS 1:6-8. **What do we learn about how the Thessalonians received the gospel?**

What followed their response to suffering? What does this teach us about how our faith in suffering can impact others?

How has the suffering of someone you know (or read about) impacted your faith?

I've mentioned Joni Eareckson Tada several times because her story of God's faithfulness in her suffering changed my life. She endures suffering without bitterness because her life is rooted in God. The source of her joy is Him, not her circumstances. When we live the same way, the world takes notice. We need not do anything else—in fact, our weakness highlights the power and sufficiency of God.

WEAKNESS HIGHLIGHTS GOD'S STRENGTH

READ 2 CORINTHIANS 12:1-10. What did Paul gain when his pleading prayer for relief was denied? How can this passage encourage you as you consider your own aches and longings?

Do you see your weakness as a strength? Have you experienced God's power more acutely in your suffering? Explain.

THE COSMIC IMPACT OF OUR WITNESS

Our glorious God, who never wastes a drop of our suffering, is using those who suffer alone to impact not only their caregivers and the few people they have contact with, but also the angels and demons who are constantly watching them respond to affliction.

When we suffer alone, we often wonder if our pain has any purpose. If no one knows what we're going through, we may wonder if there's any point to a godly response. That's what I wondered until I realized I was not alone in my suffering and that an immense invisible audience was watching my response to trials. And because of that, my response to suffering mattered.

I first heard this idea from pastor John Piper, as he unpacked the book of Job. He talked about how, in the first two chapters, we see God's glory on display for the angels and demons. They watch Job praise and honor God even after his calamity, which included losing his seven children, his possessions, and his health.[2]

God demonstrates His wisdom to the powers and principalities in the heavenly realms as they observe the church—you and me. I believe we bear witness to the greatness of God and the power of the gospel by our lives and testimony, including our response to suffering. The spirit world is looking on when we hold our tongues when we're tempted to speak unkindly. When we are racked with pain, alone, and choose to praise God anyway. When we face a demanding boss, challenging children, or a callous husband and trust God to give us the strength we need.

As we endure all these things, we show the surpassing value of Christ to the unseen, watching world.

> READ LUKE 15:7,10; EPHESIANS 3:10. What do these verses tell us about the heavenly realms? How can that be encouraging to people struggling in isolation?

Countless people with severe, life-altering diseases and disabilities live in isolation and aren't part of an earthly community, but they are surrounded by heavenly beings, a glorious cloud of witnesses, and the Lord Himself. And as they turn to God in their suffering, they glorify God before the unseen world.

These saints who live in forced isolation carry an extra burden that others do not. We may feel ill-equipped to support them, but if we have ever experienced God's comfort, we can compassionately pass that comfort on to anyone.

PASSING ON GOD'S COMFORT

> READ 2 CORINTHIANS 1:3-4. What do we learn about comfort in this passage?

How have you experienced God's comfort firsthand?

This passage says we are to comfort others with the comfort we have received. How can understanding this truth give you confidence as you minister to others?

To comfort others in their suffering, God must first comfort us. We cannot learn God's comfort secondhand; it's not found through books or classes, only through direct experience. And once we've experienced it, we can pass that abiding comfort onto others.

COMFORT THROUGH COMMUNITY

The deepest fellowship I've experienced is among other suffering believers. Though we often cannot meet each other's physical needs, we can pray—the most important work of all. Suffering saints can minister to others by voicing how the Spirit has comforted them—through answered prayers, encouraging Scriptures, inspiring articles, and stories of God's sustaining grace. While meeting in person is wonderful, with technology we can minister to others and be ministered to by saints across the world.

READ COLOSSIANS 3:12-17. List all the ways you can encourage others in your community, even when you're suffering.

Which of these are you currently practicing? In what areas do you need to grow?

The apostle Paul wrote the New Testament epistles Ephesians, Philippians, Colossians, and Philemon from prison. He was chained and needed people to physically help meet his needs, probably including the writing of these letters. Yet his impact from prison was incalculable as he shared the gospel, prayed for others, passed on what God was teaching him, and encouraged both the people around him and the recipients of his letters.

READ COLOSSIANS 4:2-13. What did Paul ask people to pray for him (vv. 3-4)?

What do Paul's words indicate believers in fellowship do for each other (vv. 7-13)?

Where in your life can you apply what you've learned about community in suffering?

DAY 3

We've looked closely at John 4 and now let's listen to the passage being read. Let the Holy Spirit speak to you through His Word another way.

Begin with prayer:

Dear Lord, speak to me through Your Word and show me something of Yourself that I need to see. Help me to clear away all distractions and let Your Word, which is living and active, penetrate my heart that I would encounter You.

Use an audio Bible app or website to listen to John 4:1-30,39-42 being read aloud. (The YouVersion Bible app, Dwell Bible app, the her.bible website, and biblegateway.com are a few options.)

As you listen, put yourself in the scene. What phrases do you notice? What do you see? Write anything that speaks to you from hearing the passage.

How has this Scripture affected the way you view suffering and community?

How do you see Jesus differently from studying this story?

Church wounds cut deep. We left a church years ago over concerns with the leadership and were surprised at the unkind remarks and rumors that began circulating about us. We loved that community, but soon friends became distant and our memories almost rewritten. It was both confusing and consuming.

I wrote in a journal entry:

> *My reputation is horrible . . . I confess I can't get this situation out of my mind. Teach me what I need to learn. Help me to let this go and keep me from bitterness . . .*

It was hard to get involved and rebuild at a new church. We finally settled in, but eventually there was hurt at this church too. We were members there when my husband left our family, causing speculation about my authenticity and character. Some people questioned whether I was still qualified to teach Bible study. When I heard the rumors about me, I wanted to pull away, feeling betrayed by people whom I'd trusted.

At the same time, I knew I couldn't do life alone. I had physical struggles—a weak body and mounting demands as a single parent. Emotionally, I needed friends to walk with us and help our lives feel normal again. I also needed spiritual encouragement to keep trusting God when I didn't feel like it. The body of Christ came through. God brought friends to lift me up and even point out how I was ministering to them in my pain.

A few journal entries from that time read:

> *On Friday, Margaret said that my faith and transparency had impacted her and deepened her faith. I'm grateful for community, and I realize how much I want words of encouragement to help me press on . . . Shalini says I encourage her by my faith which seems crazy because she is the one who encourages me . . . And then this week so many people have confirmed a calling on me to write—Debby, Bill, and Paula all separately told me the same thing. Maybe You will use what I have been through to minister to others . . .*

God encouraged me through fellow believers, especially my sister, who constantly reminded me of God's love and my value. Through tears, my weekly prayer group interceded for me. I felt glimmers of hope when they suggested this painful time could forge a new ministry.

People from church changed light bulbs, chauffeured my daughters, and organized prayer. At one point, a dozen people gathered in our bonus room, read through Psalm 107 together, lamented with me, and prayed over my practical requests. These friends reassured me that God would never leave me, that they were faithfully praying for me, and that I was a valuable part of the community, even when I had nothing to give.

> While we are all both sufferers and helpers in different contexts, for this next exercise, read through both categories, but choose one to act on. Schedule your planned actions within the next two weeks if possible.

CATEGORY ONE: You are currently suffering and need help.

Pray:

> *Lord, I come to You with many needs, unsure of how or if they can be met. I ask You to open my eyes to see what I need and how You might be providing for me even now. Give me discernment about who to call for help and give me grace to put aside my pride and past hurts and trust You in this. Help me to recognize that even if people can't help me or can only do a little, You will provide for my needs.*

> In a perfect world, how would you like the community around you to help you? List everything you can think of, including physical help, emotional support, and spiritual encouragement.

List a few friends and prayerfully consider who to reach out to first. Ask if they can meet for an hour—preferably in person, but otherwise over the phone or video.

At the meeting, share your needs and specific ways they can help. Or maybe just use the time to brainstorm ideas of how other people could help meet your needs. Note here what you want to discuss.

CATEGORY TWO: Someone in need comes to mind or you are not in a season of need yourself

Pray:

Lord, I don't know how or where You want to use me, but I bring my empty, open hands. Make me attentive to Your voice and help me step out of my comfort zone in faith. Remove my fears of being inadequate or too busy and help me trust that You will equip me with everything I need. Show me who to call.

What resources do you have that God could use to meet the needs of someone who is suffering? Think of physical resources, talents, and spiritual gifts. How has God used you in the past?

Write the names of a few friends in need and ask the Lord to show you the person to contact.

Contact them and consider saying: *The Lord brought you to mind. I would love to get together to check-in, to listen, to pray, and to see how I might help. Would you be willing to get together with me for an hour?*

Try to meet in person, but if not, meet by phone or video. When you meet, primarily listen. Just your presence and attention will minister to the person in need. Pray with your friends in the moment and pledge to continue to pray. Ask them to share with you specific prayer needs as they arise. If appropriate, put together a "care" plan and involve other friends to help carry the load. Consider writing the person an encouraging letter, note, or text within the next few days.

After your conversation—whether you met with someone in need or asked for help—record what happened.

What about the meeting was easier than you anticipated? What was more challenging?

How do you need to follow up?

DAY 4

Some people have the gift of encouragement, while others . . . not so much. My children are usually in the latter category. Here is an excerpt from our 2014 Christmas letter:

> *Yesterday Kristi told me I needed to stop wearing my old coat because it looked awful. Minutes later, she noticed my new shoes and said they were cool. But before I could bask in the unsolicited praise, she added, "I like them because from the knees down, you look like a little old man."*

I'm thankful that God gives us people, besides our children, to encourage us. Especially when we are struggling. God's gift of community can be life-giving, both for the people who are suffering and those who minister to them.

READ 2 KINGS 4:1-7. What was the woman's situation, and who initiated the conversation about her need (v. 1)?

Summarize Elisha's instructions (vv. 2-4).

How did the widow receive help? What role did the woman's sons play? What role did her neighbors play? What can you learn from this interplay of responsibility? Who ultimately provided for her?

While the help of the son and neighbors made it possible for her to meet her needs, it was the Lord who set this in motion. It is His work that makes our help helpful.

What's your initial response when others ask you for help? What requests are easy for you? What requests make you uncomfortable? What are your fears in being asked to help?

How do you feel about asking others for help? What are the benefits? What types of requests are easy to make? What are some difficult asks? What are your fears in asking?

ASKING FOR HELP

I don't like asking for help. It's hard and humbling. So I'm reluctant to ask, even when it's for something important. The reason for my hesitation has varied through different seasons of life, but I've discovered that it's often rooted in pride, fear, or resentment. So as you answer the question on the next page, please know I'm not coming from a place of judgment or condemnation but rather a desire to offer help and healing from what I've learned.

Before doing the following exercise, ask the Lord to open your eyes to truth, to help you not be defensive, and to act on what He reveals.

Which of the following have kept you from asking for help from people in your church or community? Circle all that apply and star the top one or two.

Fear of being rejected or judged (1 Sam. 16:7; Prov. 29:25; Rom. 8:1)

Fear of being a burden or looking needy. Wanting to be self-sufficient (2 Cor. 12:9; Gal. 6:2)

Resentment that others haven't shown up for you as you have for them (Prov. 19:11; 1 Cor. 13:5; Heb. 12:1)

Past hurts, including church hurt (Isa. 43:18-19; Phil. 3:13-14; Col. 3:12-13)

Feeling envy over seeing others have what you long for (Prov. 14:30; Rom. 12:15; 1 Cor. 13:4)

Other

_____

_____

_____

_____

Don't have a church community (Heb. 10:24-25)

Look up the Scriptures listed beside the reason(s) you most identify with. How do those passages apply to your situation? What steps might God be calling you to take in response?

SHARING OUR NEEDS

The Lord is the One who ultimately meets our needs, just as He did for the widow in 2 Kings. But He did use people to fulfill those needs. We can feel vulnerable letting others know where we need help, but they won't know unless we tell them. The acronym **SHARE** can guide you as you consider asking for help.

S – Seek the Lord's direction on how others can help (Ps. 25:9; Jas. 1:5).

+ Pray for the Lord's wisdom and direction about your true needs and who to reach out to.

H – Honestly tell people what is happening, even if it feels humbling (Prov. 15:33; 1 Pet. 5:5).

+ People are more likely to be there for you when they know you need help.

A – Ask specifically for what you need or want (Jas. 5:14-15).

+ The more specific we are about our desires and requests, the easier it is for people to respond.

R – Respect their limitations, understanding that God ultimately provides for you (Phil. 4:19).

+ Understanding that people may be unavailable or unable to help provide what we need is critical.

E – Encourage them as they encourage you (Rom. 1:11-12).

+ Share how God is meeting your needs through them. Tell them about God's faithfulness to you.

The apostle Paul was a great example of how to deal with needs; he prayed about everything, honestly made known what he needed, and asked for specific help. He didn't want to overburden anyone and reminded the churches that God would bless them for their generosity. He also constantly prayed for them, which he mentioned frequently in his letters.

Like Paul, expect God to meet all your needs, using others as He chooses. Don't assume any one person can do everything. First give your concerns to the Lord (1 Pet. 5:7) who knows what you're lacking, and He will supply it (Matt. 6:30-33).

READ ROMANS 12:4-18. List all the principles of community you see in this passage. What things on the list are you doing well? Where are you lacking? What can you do to strengthen your weak areas?

SERVING OTHERS

Our daily lives involve lack in some areas and surplus in others. We may feel overwhelmed caring for a newborn baby but have time to pray at night when we're up feeding her. Even in our own suffering, we can pay attention to those around us who are hurting. Don't feel like you need to provide for all of their needs. But the Lord may ask you to do something. The acronym **SHOW UP** can help you remember how to be there for people.

S – Show up (Job 2:11; Gal. 6:9; Heb. 10:24-25).

- Our presence is often our best gift. Words are not required. Just be there, especially when you say you will.

H – How is *today* (Phil. 4:10)?

- Asking about how someone is doing "today" is an easier question to answer than the general "how are you?" It communicates care.

O – Offer specific help (Rom. 12:13; 1 Pet. 4:10).

- Be as specific as possible. For example, "I have Thursday from two to four free. Can I run some errands for you?"

W – Words of encouragement—spoken or written (1 Sam. 23:16; 1 Thess. 5:11).

- Affirm people. Call, text, or write a note. Sometimes I just text Scripture and let them know I'm praying.

U – Use active listening (Jas. 1:19).

- Give people space to talk and don't sermonize or minimize their pain. Listen more than you speak.

P – Pray (1 Thess. 5:17; Jas. 5:16).

- Prayer is the best thing we can do. Pray *for* them. Pray *with* them. And be open to letting God use you to be the answer to your prayers.

Bonus Study

THE BODY OF CHRIST

READ 1 CORINTHIANS 12:12-13,18-27. Do you see yourself as interconnected to others in the church? Why or why not?

What parts of the body are indispensable (v. 22)? How can that relate to someone who is suffering? Who might that be in your church?

How does the joy or sorrow of one member of the body impact the rest (v. 26)? How have you experienced this in your church from either perspective? Explain.

You are seen, known, and loved by the Lord. Christ uses His body—other believers in the church—to encourage us and show us His love. We in turn, glorify God as we trust and praise Him through adversity. We can be assured that God has a purpose for our suffering—for His glory and our eternal joy.

DAY 5

We started this week asking the big question: *How can God use my suffering if I feel useless?* How has this week's study helped answer that question? Explain.

How have you experienced God's love and faithfulness toward you this week? Where have you sensed His presence? Pay attention to signs of His love and presence through specific incidents like answers to prayer, unexpected peace, or comfort after reading Scripture.

How is God working in you? In your suffering? Where have you seen hints of His purpose?

READ 1 PETER 4:8-11. How does this passage relate to what we've studied this week?

Have you ever experienced God's comfort? If so, what has that looked like for you? How can you share that comfort with someone else?

Try to fill in the SHARE and SHOW UP acronyms from memory. If you need to, review that section (pages 147–148) and the corresponding Scriptures.

S

H

A

R

E

S

H

O

W

U

P

Read the following statements about our purpose in community and how God wants us to encourage one another. Choose one statement, look up the verse, write the verse on a sticky note or note card, and put it in a prominent place to help remind you of how we need one another.

Each of us has a purpose, role, and place of belonging in the body of Christ.
READ ROMANS 12:4-5.

God calls us to encourage each other.
READ 1 THESSALONIANS 5:11.

We are to carry one another's burdens.
READ GALATIANS 6:2.

We can encourage each other through Scripture, song, and fellowship.
READ COLOSSIANS 3:16.

Don't stop meeting with other believers. We need each other.
READ HEBREWS 10:24-25.

Final Thought

Our suffering has purpose and can bring God glory as friends encourage us in our suffering and we in turn encourage others. That encouragement comes as we bear witness to God's goodness and faithfulness and tangibly support those in need. This session focused on reaching out in specific, practical ways to encourage someone else, or letting your needs be known so you can be encouraged by others. What were you able to do? Have you told anyone your story of God's faithfulness? Have you mentioned your needs or reached out to someone else in need? Have you shared with anyone how God has comforted you in your struggle? If not, reach out to someone now. After you've done that, journal how God has met you through the process. What have you learned?

SESSION 6:

HOW CAN GOD USE MY SUFFERING WHEN I FEEL USELESS?

Watch the Session 6 video and take notes below.

GROUP DISCUSSION / QUESTIONS FOR REFLECTION

What part of the video teaching was most significant for you? Why?

How has your faith been strengthened by watching the way a fellow believer handles her suffering?

In your difficult times, who has been there for you and how have they lifted you up?

What are some things that hinder or limit your willingness to help someone who is suffering?

What is corporate lament, and how is that helpful to those who are suffering?

How has your view of suffering been affected by what you've learned today?

What's one thing you've learned this week of study that better equips you to help others who are suffering?

To access the video teaching sessions, use the instructions in the back of your Bible study book.

Question

WHAT IF THIS NEVER GETS BETTER?

DAY 1

While I know that heaven is going to be an amazing place, it's hard to imagine what it will be like. We just can't understand some things until we see them. My daughter Katie would agree. Here's an excerpt from our Christmas letter when she was three years old.

We've been teaching Katie about Jesus, telling her that Jesus is always here with us. Just when we thought it was sinking in, we had this conversation:

Katie: "Mommy, did you say Jesus is always with us?"
Vaneetha: "Yes, Katie, that's right!"
Katie: "Well, He's not here now. If He was, His car would be outside."

Maybe you can relate. It's sometimes hard to believe or get excited about things that aren't observable. So much of what we believe in is invisible—even the core of our belief rests in what we hope for and cannot see. The faith needed to be certain of those things comes from knowing God and trusting in His goodness. We are presently called to wait patiently, knowing that one day our faith will become sight when we'll see all God's promises fulfilled.

Last week we talked about how God uses others to encourage us and how we in turn can encourage them. Sharing with others how Jesus has met us in our suffering is a powerful witness, demonstrating the surpassing value of Christ.

This week we are talking about my third and final 3 Ps anchor—*the PROMISE of heaven.* Heaven anchors our hope in eternity where something infinitely better awaits us all. This is critical to remember since some losses and longings will last a lifetime, as we'll see in Leah's life. She never received what she longed for, yet God became enough for her. And through her came a greater blessing which she did not see—from the line of her son Judah came King David, and later King Jesus.

READ GENESIS 29:16-35. What stands out to you in this passage? Pay attention to Leah's pain and longings in her marriage to Jacob. Is there anything surprising to you? Explain.

REREAD GENESIS 29:16-30. What do we find out early on (vv. 16-18) that sets the stage for a story of rivalry and comparison?

What emotions do you think Leah experienced? Whom would you have been most upset with? Laban, her father? Jacob, her husband? Rachel, her sister? Explain.

From the author's comparison of the sisters and Jacob's declaration of love for Rachel, we sense that pain is ahead for Leah. Her struggles were layered— her father's deception, her husband's response, and her sister's preferential treatment. I wonder if she felt safe to talk to anyone about her pain since it all came from her family.

Rachel was clearly a knockout, beautiful in form and appearance, while Leah's eyes were described as "weak" or "soft." The Hebrew word used here is difficult to translate. It could be a positive description, indicating Leah's eyes were tender or lovely, perhaps reflective of a quieter personality. But the contrasting feel of the passage likely indicates it was a negative description.[1] Whatever their differences, Rachel was Jacob's type, and Leah was not. The description of Jacob's feelings in verse 30 almost brings me to tears as I remember all the times I've felt unloved and "not enough" by people whose approval and love I've longed for.

Have you ever felt unloved or "less than" in comparison to others? Explain. How do you respond when you feel that way? Take a few minutes and talk to the Lord about it.

REREAD GENESIS 29:31-35. Many names in the Bible are significant, reflecting both the mindset of the person doing the naming as well as the character of the person being named.

List the names of Leah's first four sons in order and why she chose those names.

NAME	REASON FOR THE NAME

What do you notice about the progression of their names? What does that tell you about Leah's mindset? Can you relate to her thinking? How?

Leah was implying through the names of her first three sons, "I am seen and heard by God so I will get what I'm longing for." Yet she did not. Jacob's feelings remained unchanged. Leah kept hoping that her next son would change the situation. I've done something similar, desperately searching for a solution that will turn my sorrow around, bringing happiness and relief. Yet as Leah named Judah, she was content that God saw her, knew her, and loved her.

Where in your life are you longing for change? Where are you wondering "What if this never gets better?" Is there something specific you're hoping will change the situation?

Pour out your ache to God. Ask Him for wisdom and direction as you move forward, remembering nothing is impossible with God.

God may eventually give you what you've been longing for. But for now, maybe He's encouraging you to keep asking, seeking, and knocking. Conversely, He may not fulfill your good desires in this life. Does your happiness depend on getting what you're hoping for, or can you be satisfied if it never changes? I've wondered that for myself.

Naming her fourth son Judah showed that Leah was able to put her identity in God and not in Jacob's love. She could praise God in the cavernous gap between her dreams and reality, allowing God to meet her in her unfulfilled longings.

As my friend Paula Rinehart says, we all have "a chosen ache—meaning not that I'd choose it, but I'm making choices to accept its presence as something that God has allowed for His own reasons—which must be good ones because He is good. . . . If I'm honest, I see with irony that my chosen aches are the very places where Christ has become real for me . . . where His forgiveness and love and power actually captured my heart."[2]

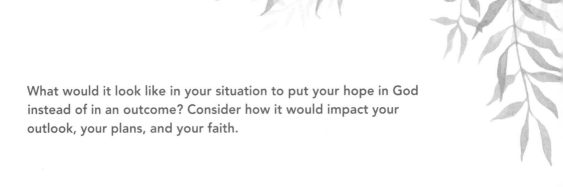

What would it look like in your situation to put your hope in God instead of in an outcome? Consider how it would impact your outlook, your plans, and your faith.

How have your longings influenced your relationship with God?

READ GENESIS 30:20. What does this verse tell us about Leah's heart after bearing Jacob two more sons?

We saw Leah's outlook shift when Judah was born, yet here she went back to yearning for Jacob's love.

Is her vacillation discouraging to you? Why or why not? How might it also be encouraging?

It's okay to mourn your losses. John Piper says, "Occasionally weep deeply over the life you hoped would be. Grieve the losses. Then wash your face. Trust God. And embrace the life you have."[3]

Leah may have grieved her longing for Jacob's love all her life. Perhaps she went back and forth, between being satisfied in God and wanting her husband's approval, as we often do with desires we wrestle with. Our lives are often a mixture of loss and longings—aches that we take to God and those we try to fulfill ourselves. Yet even in that vacillation, we can be assured that we are extravagantly loved by God.

Leah's story feels tender to me. I told my ex-husband during his affair that I felt like Leah to him—the wife of obligation, someone he never had passion for. I couldn't explain at the time how devastating that comparison felt to me, but in my husband's rejection, Jesus's love became more precious to me.

As I mentioned earlier, Judah, Leah's fourth son, is the line of David and therefore the line of Christ. She wanted to be loved and honored by Jacob, but instead she was loved and honored by God for all eternity. Through Leah's line came the salvation of the world.

> **How does Leah's life and legacy encourage you in your situation right now?**

DAY 2

Early in Acts we get a front row seat to Stephen's life and especially his death. He was selected as a deacon, being described as a man "full of faith and of the Holy Spirit" (Acts 6:5). God used him mightily in the early church (Acts 6:8), and no one could match his wisdom (Acts 6:10). Naturally, we'd assume that he would have had a long and fruitful life leading the church and bringing people to Jesus. But that wasn't Stephen's story.

Some of the Jews were opposed to Stephen's words and works, so they falsely accused him and dragged him before the Sanhedrin (Jewish ruling council). Stephen answered their accusations with a long sermon reciting the history of Israel, accusing the Jewish leaders of being stiff-necked, resisting the Holy Spirit, and murdering Jesus (Acts 7:51-53). As you can imagine, this further enraged his audience.

> READ ACTS 7:54–8:4. What did Stephen see when he gazed into heaven (vv. 55-56)? Do you find anything in this account encouraging or surprising? Explain.

Scripture generally depicts Jesus seated at the right hand of God (Eph. 1:20; Heb. 12:2), yet in this passage, Stephen saw Jesus standing at God's right hand. Scholars debate why the different posture for Jesus, but it could have been to welcome Stephen as he entered heaven.

> What words does your Bible use to indicate that Stephen was dead (v. 60)?

The apostle Paul also used that term for death (1 Cor. 15:20; 1 Thess. 4:13). Is that term comforting to you? Explain.

Peter Marshall, who was a chaplain of the U.S. Senate, told the story of a young boy who was dying from an incurable illness and asked his mother, "What is it like to die? Does it hurt?"

The mother prayed for wisdom to know how to answer. She told her son it was like what happened when, after playing hard and being so tired, he would fall asleep in his parents' bed. Then his father would come when he was sleeping and carry him back in his own room. She said, "Kenneth, death is like that. We just wake up one morning to find ourselves in the other room; our own room where we belong because the Lord Jesus loved us." The explanation comforted the little boy and took away his fears. Several weeks later, he fell asleep.[4]

Not everyone faces death as gently as this young boy. Some people experience excruciating and abrupt deaths as Stephen did. But regardless, those who know Christ will see Jesus waiting for them as they fall asleep.

What resulted from Stephen's death (8:1,4)? How does that help put his death in a larger context?

The church scattered, and the gospel spread after Stephen's death. Like the book of Acts, the New Testament letters encouraged sufferers with a message of endurance, purpose, and heavenly reward with little mention of relief or rescue. The writer of Hebrews described people of faith as those not looking for an earthly kingdom but rather a heavenly one (Heb. 11:16) where they would receive an unfading reward (Heb. 11:26). They were tortured, whipped, imprisoned, and stoned, knowing they would rise again to a better life with unending glory in heaven (Heb. 11:35-40). The Bible assures us that there will be rewards in heaven—praise, honor, and glory—for people who have persevered and clung to Christ in their suffering.

The apostle Peter wrote his first letter to the persecuted church, knowing how intensely his readers were suffering. He knew many of them would lose their lives for the gospel like Stephen.

READ 1 PETER 1:3-7. List everything we are assured of when we are born again. What assurance is most meaningful to you and why?

What did Peter say about their trials in verse 6?

Peter says here and in 5:10 that their trials would only last "a little while" (or "short time"), fully aware his readers' intense trials could last their entire lifetimes. Peter was not downplaying how long they'd suffer, but rather contrasting their suffering with eternity. Putting it in perspective, our time on earth represents a fraction of an inch compared to a ten thousand mile journey. Or a tiny blip on an unending time line graph.

Does that comparison make enduring your present trials easier? Why or why not?

Secondly, Peter described their trials as "necessary," meaning they weren't the results of fate, chance, or being in the wrong place at the wrong time. Rather, they came because of the will of God.[5]

How can knowing that our trials are necessary be helpful?

What does verse 7 say will be the result of our trials now and into eternity?

READ JAMES 1:2-4 (OR REVIEW YOUR NOTES FROM SESSION 5, DAY 4) AND JAMES 1:12 ALONG WITH 2 CORINTHIANS 4:16-18. What truths are echoed in 1 Peter 1:6-7? What encourages you from these passages?

On earth we have God's presence, but heaven surpasses anything we've ever experienced on earth. Since heaven holds incomparable joy, it is far better to die and be with Christ (Phil. 1:21-23); death has no sting for us (1 Cor. 15:54-55).

Heaven is where people who have accepted Christ go when they die to spend eternity with God. While all of heaven will be incredible and we won't be encumbered by the effects of sin, the most spectacular part of heaven will be having unbroken, face-to-face fellowship with God forever.

While we have a limited understanding of heaven, here are my thoughts on some important questions.

WHY SHOULD I CARE ABOUT HEAVEN NOW?

Believing in heaven is central to our faith. If heaven wasn't real, our hope would be completely misplaced (1 Cor. 15:14,17-20). We can press on through intense suffering when we're convinced that something magnificent is coming.

> **READ 1 CORINTHIANS 2:9.** Is this passage comforting to you? Explain.

God is using your suffering to prepare you for heaven and incomparable glory. Your affliction may not seem light or momentary—it may feel unspeakably heavy and may have lasted a lifetime—but it is brief compared to eternity. Your pain will not last forever.

Sam Gamgee's question toward the end of J. R. R. Tolkien's *The Return of the King* embodies the unexpected appearance of goodness and joy when he asked Gandalf: "Is everything sad going to come untrue?"[6] The answer for us is a resounding "Yes!" Everything sad will come untrue as God shows us how all things were working for our good. C. S. Lewis echoed this idea that heaven will heal everything when he said: "[People] say of some temporal suffering, 'No future bliss can make up for it' not knowing that heaven, once attained, will work backwards and turn even that agony into a glory."[7]

God will turn our agonies into glory in heaven when He makes all things new. What a glorious truth. As Randy Alcorn says, "'They all lived happily ever after' is not merely a fairy tale. It's the blood-bought promise of God for all who trust in the gospel."[8]

WHAT WILL HEAVEN BE LIKE?

Perhaps many of us see ourselves joining angels sitting on clouds playing harps when we think about heaven, which doesn't sound like an appealing way to spend eternity. But heaven will be more like going home. We will no longer be tempted by sin, and we will have new bodies and minds that will delight in God forever.

Randy Alcorn says this about heaven:

Our belief that heaven will be boring betrays a heresy—that God Himself is boring. There's no greater nonsense. Our desire for pleasure and the experience of joy come directly from God's hand. He made our taste buds, adrenaline, and the nerve endings that convey pleasure to our brains. Likewise, our imaginations and capacity for joy were made by the God whom some imagine is boring. Are we so arrogant as to imagine that human beings came up with the idea of having fun? [9]

READ REVELATION 21:1-6. What is our relationship with God going to be in heaven, and what will He do for us there?

What are you most looking forward to in heaven? What are you most excited about being made new?

The rest of Revelation 21–22 gives us a picture of the new heaven and the new earth, with dazzling beauty and a river of life, and no tarnish from our sin and selfishness. It will be an unending celebration where we won't be tempted, afraid, or dissatisfied and will fully appreciate all of God's gifts. Everything we love on earth will be magnified beyond our comprehension; heaven will be better than anything we've experienced.

WHAT IF I DIE PREMATURELY?

We cannot die before our time. Each of us will live every day that God has ordained for us from before the foundation of the world. Our exact days are numbered by God who will make sure we've accomplished all He has for us to do.

How do the following Scriptures affirm that truth?

◆ Psalm 139:16

◆ Philippians 1:6

What seems random to us is not random to God, for there is nothing random in the universe. If we believe we can die prematurely, we will live in fear of doing anything since we don't know where it might lead. Yet, as we saw in Session Four, nothing happens outside of God's sovereign will.

HOW SHOULD WE LIVE WHEN WE KNOW WE'RE DYING?

Several years ago, I received a letter that Becky, a woman with metastatic cancer, had written to encourage a friend who was newly diagnosed with cancer. This was Becky's (abbreviated) battle plan:

1. Recognizing that most of our battles are waged in the mind, I choose to focus on God who knew before the foundation of the world that I would have cancer and has already provided the resources I need to face it.

2. I chose to view this illness as a gift. It is a time to draw near to God, to experience God more fully, to enjoy the simple joys of life, to focus on those things that are truly important.

3. Although cancer wants to be an all-encompassing issue in my life, I refuse to sink within myself. I will reach out to someone else each day with a letter, word of encouragement, act of service, or prayer.

4. I will not ignore my emotions. I will allow myself to cry as necessary in order to vent my feelings, but I will NOT be ruled by them.

5. I will share what is happening with others and enlist their support and prayers.

6. I will make both short-term and long-term goals in order to have something to look forward to. I will endeavor to keep my life as "normal" as possible as long as I am physically able.

7. I will find some reason to laugh every day.

8. I will remind myself that, in some inexplicable way, the way I conduct myself during this time of struggle does impact the spiritual world.

What in Becky's battle plan is most meaningful to you? What will you incorporate into your life and current situation?

DAY 3

We've looked at parts of Leah's life in Genesis. Now let's listen to her story being read and let the Holy Spirit speak through His Word another way.

Let's pray:

Dear Lord, speak to me through Your Word and show me something of Yourself that I need to see. Help me to clear away all distractions and let Your Word, which is living and active, penetrate my heart that I would encounter You.

Use an audio Bible app or website to listen to Genesis 29:16-35 being read aloud. (The YouVersion Bible app, Dwell Bible app, the her.bible website, and biblegateway.com are a few options.)

As you listen, put yourself in the scene. What phrases do you notice? What do you see? Write anything that speaks to you from hearing the passage.

How has this Scripture affected your view of your own loss and longings?

How do you see the Lord differently from studying this story?

This final week's study is close to my heart. As I write this, I'm struggling with the effects of post-polio syndrome—increasing pain in my right shoulder and arm and profound weakness which has left me struggling to hold a pen. Since my left arm is now nonfunctional, my right arm is all I have left. The doctors said this would eventually happen, but it always felt far away. Now it's all too real. I know that God can miraculously heal me and I'm praying that He will, yet I also know that physical healing may not be God's best for me.

This gradual loss of my strength, which is trickling away, is difficult. My life and energy are measured by teaspoons, not by cups like they used to be, or gallons that others seem to have. I am not embracing, loving, or finding joy in the loss itself, but I am embracing, loving, and finding joy in God as I surrender it to Him.

This wrestling with loss and trust isn't new. Eleven years ago, I wrote this:

> *I can't move my left arm, and as I write this, I have a burning pain in my shoulder. Am I seeing my strength peter out, slowly draining all my energy and leaving me with nothing? Will You restore me to health? Just when I get used to a new level of hard, another comes tripping along beside it, knocking it over and overtaking it all. Where do I need to trust You more? Help me to press deeper into You as I surrender this.*

> *There are other losses I haven't seen turn around or been tied up with a shiny bow. When I go to my son Paul's grave, it's a constant reminder that I will not be reunited with him until heaven. My marriage ended in divorce a decade ago when I so wanted a different ending.*

I wrote about my failing marriage in a journal entry after my husband left:

> *I want a bow. I want to live happily ever after in this life. But I know that life may not be restored the way I want it to be. Regardless, none of it will be wasted. Lord, make my suffering count for something.*

> *Let grief and pain do their work in my life. Deliverance may be in the next life only. The immediate relief of my suffering should not be my end goal. My hope is not in an outcome. My hope is solely in You.*

God provided Joel, an incredible man, to be my second husband. I thank God daily for him. Yet even the bow that God gave me in Joel will not last forever, as nothing in life can. Everything in this world will pass away because something much better is coming.

These words from Samuel Rutherford encouraged me this morning as I struggled to write this section:

> *If God had told me some time ago that He was about to make me as happy as*
> *I could be in this world, and then had told me that He should begin by crippling me*
> *in all my limbs, and removing me from all my usual sources of enjoyment, I should*
> *have thought it a very strange mode of accomplishing His purpose. And yet, how is*
> *His manifold wisdom even in this! For if you should see a man shut up in a closed*
> *room, idolizing a set of lamps and rejoicing in their light, and you wished to make*
> *him truly happy, you would begin by blowing out all his lamps, and then throw*
> *open the shutters to let in the light of heaven.*[10]

Earlier in the study I asked you to make a list of the positive and negative events in your life on pages 186–187. Review the lists. Make sure you've included all your important events, successes and failures, joys and sorrows, and happiest moments as well as your deep hurts and disappointments.

We are going to graph the events on a time line of your life (pages 188–189). The beginning of the graph will represent your birth and the end of the graph your current age. Chronologically plot each event with a dot. Write a key word or two to remind you of the event. The positive events go above the line and the negative ones go below the line. The happiest moments should be the highest points and the saddest moments the lowest. Then connect all the points.

As you look at your graph, write down what is stirring in you. Do you see patterns or themes? Explain.

Remember that Jesus was with you through all you went through, even though you may not have realized it. Picture Him with you during the most difficult times.

Were there times you remember His presence? Explain.

We know that God uses pain for our good and His glory. Where do you see glimpses of His purposes as you reflect on your suffering?

Now, turn your graph upside down. What do you notice?
Do your lowest, most difficult times correlate with growth in your spiritual life? Explain.

When I did this exercise for the first time, I was astonished at how the hardest moments in my life all drew me closer to God than I could have imagined. From my lowest emotional points came my most significant growth, my greatest dependence on God, and my platform for ministry. It was in these low points that God did His deepest work in me. The gap between my dreams and reality was where I had the deepest communion with God.

Has your experience been similar to mine? Explain.

Write everything you learned from this exercise. How has it helped you? Where has it discouraged you? Spend a few minutes talking to God about this.

DAY 4

We're going to wrap up this week of study today so we can do a review of the whole study tomorrow.

We started this week asking the big question: *What if this never gets better?* How has this week's study helped answer that question? Explain.

How have you experienced God's love and faithfulness toward you this week? Where have you sensed His presence? Pay attention to signs of His love and presence through specific incidents like answers to prayer, unexpected peace, and comfort after reading Scripture.

How is God working in you? In your suffering? Where have you seen hints of His purpose?

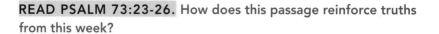

READ PSALM 73:23-26. How does this passage reinforce truths from this week?

In what ways do you need to bring your longings to God, rather than stuffing them down, trying to control them, or wishing they would go away?

Where have you put your hope if not in the love and presence of God?

Elisabeth Elliot said: "Of one thing I am perfectly sure: God's story never ends with ashes."[11] What does she mean, and how does that comfort you in the face of your suffering?

Choose one statement about our glorious future, look up the verse, and write it on a sticky note or index card. Put it in a prominent place to help remind you of our temporary suffering and our hope in heaven.

We will forget all the troubles of this earth in heaven.
READ ISAIAH 65:17.

Jesus has prepared an incredible home for us in heaven and will take us there Himself.
READ JOHN 14:1-3.

What we're suffering now is nothing compared to the glory we'll see in heaven.
READ ROMANS 8:18.

There's no way for us to comprehend all that God has in store for those who love Him.
READ 1 CORINTHIANS 2:9.

Christ has work for us while on earth but dying and being with Him will be better.
READ PHILIPPIANS 1:21-22.

DAY 5

It's hard to believe that this is our last day together. It's been such a privilege to walk through these weeks with you, sharing what the Lord has taught me through my losses and longings and hopefully encouraging you in your own trials.

Each week we looked at one of the 3 Ps anchors I cling to in pain. Combined they form a framework that has helped me make sense of suffering when life falls apart. These anchors are:

1. The **Presence** of God

2. God's **Purpose** in suffering

3. The **Promise** of heaven

In Sessions 2–4, we focused on God's presence in suffering. We looked at God's love for us—a love too deep to fully understand but never failing. We talked about connecting with God through prayer and reading Scripture and finding joy in Him alone. Since God is always with us, we can have peace in any situation, knowing He will give us exactly what we need.

In Sessions 5–6, we learned that our suffering has purpose. Our sovereign God uses everything in our lives for our good and His glory. We talked about how God uses our pain to help us rely on Him, which refines our character and produces endurance. We saw how God encourages us through community and we in turn can encourage and comfort others. In Session 7, we focused on the promise of heaven—our sure hope that our pain will end in glory.

Here's a more detailed look at the breathtaking gifts associated with each P:

PRESENCE

SESSION 2	SESSION 3	SESSION 4
Assurance you are deeply loved	Inspiration and delight from the Word	Love that casts out fear
Indescribable intimacy	Freedom to be vulnerable and honest	Reassurance that He will never leave you
Confidence that God sees and knows everything about you	His listening ear whenever you call	Provision for everything you need
	The assurance of wisdom and guidance	A peace that passes understanding
Certainty that God is FOR you	Joy in God's presence	

PURPOSE

SESSION 5	SESSION 6
Perseverance in trials	God's comfort in your suffering
Character that reflects Christ	A testimony with credibility and power
Faith refined by fire	A witness that draws others to Christ
Assurance your suffering is not wasted	The privilege of encouraging others
	The opportunity to glorify God through pain

PROMISE OF HEAVEN

SESSION 7
Crowns in heaven
A weight of glory beyond all comparison
No more suffering or sin
Eternity with happily ever after
Unending and uninterrupted joy in God

As you look over these stunning assurances:

Put a "✓" by the ones most meaningful to you. If applicable, note when you have experienced them in your life. Take a moment to thank God for these gifts.

Put a "~" by the ones that feel distant and don't seem to apply to you. Why do you think they don't feel applicable? Ask God to show you how they are true in your life.

Put a "++" by the ones you want to experience more fully in this life. What might a more meaningful experience look like? Ask God to deepen your experience with them.

These 3 Ps are woven throughout Scripture. Romans 8 is a glorious chapter in Scripture that beautifully encapsulates them all.

> **READ ROMANS 8.** Write down all the truths and themes you notice from our Bible study. Journal your thoughts. Pay special attention to any mention of God's Presence, Purpose, and the Promise of heaven as you consider your relationship with God, the power of the Spirit, and your own suffering.

At the beginning of this study I asked you to write down your questions on page 6. Take a moment to look back at them.

Were any of your questions answered during this study? Did grappling with them move you to a deeper faith? Did God reveal any truths that have softened your uncertainties? Journal your answers. No matter what questions remain, the answer to our deepest questions can't be summarized in a paragraph; the answer lies in God Himself.

C. S. Lewis would agree. In his novel, *Till We Have Faces*, the main character, Orual, demands an answer for her multiple layers of grief and loss. But after meeting God in a vision, Orual is transformed and exclaims: "I know now, Lord, why you utter no answer. You are yourself the answer. Before your face, questions die away."[12]

Orual's experience reminds me of Job, whom we've spoken of in this study. He was a righteous man who experienced unspeakable loss. He demanded that God answer him, spewing questions like: "Why is life given to those with no future, those God has surrounded with difficulties?" and "What good will it do us to pray?" and "Why must the godly wait for him in vain?" (Job 3:23; 21:15; 24:1, NLT). Those questions feel all too familiar. They could have been mine.

God didn't answer any of Job's questions directly, but He did tell Job about His power and purposes. It was seeing God and understanding His limitless power that ultimately satisfied Job (Job 42:2,5-6). As Ron Deal says, "God doesn't defend Himself, He just defines Himself."[13] And that was enough for Job.

Like Job, meeting God in suffering has changed my questions, changed my faith, and changed my life. I'm more able to trust God with the unknowns in my life because I know He's been to tomorrow and is preparing me for it today. God's presence has become almost tangible in my pain as His comfort envelops me. I don't need answers as much as I need Jesus, so my questions have become less pressing. My fears less consuming. My need to understand less important. I can live with uncertainty knowing that I am seen, known, and loved by God who will not withhold anything good from me.

For me, everything rests on the goodness and faithfulness of God.

God's very nature, some of His essential qualities, are what we need to see in our suffering. Paul mentioned many of them in Romans 15 when he talked about "the God of endurance and encouragement" (v. 5), "the God of hope [who fills us] with joy and peace" (v. 13), concluding with "the God of peace" (v. 33). These eternal attributes shaped what we focused on each week of the study—love, joy, peace, endurance, encouragement, and hope.

We looked at God's love as we explored the grief of Mary and Martha. We saw Hannah's joy after her lament over the pain of infertility. We talked about finding peace in a storm as we saw Mary, Jesus's mother, and Mary Magdalene. We witnessed Naomi's endurance through her trials as God was working for her good. We saw how Jesus encouraged the Samaritan woman, who encouraged her community to trust Jesus. Lastly, we saw how Leah found hope in God despite her unmet longings.

As we lean into God in our suffering, these attributes of love, joy, peace, endurance, encouragement, and hope—characteristics of a Spirit-filled life—will be increasingly evident in our lives. We will become more like Christ the more we keep our eyes on Him.

Suffering can open up a deeper life with the Lord. As you look at your suffering, what do you know about God because of it? Do you sense His presence even in the mess? How is He reshaping you?

My relationship with God was once focused on Him fixing the problem, changing the situation, making the pain stop, or delivering me from my trials. That's all I prayed about because all I wanted was relief. Yet as I was waiting, God offered me something far better and more satisfying than relief—an encounter with Him. That intimacy with God has led to a more fulfilling, richer life in Him than I could have ever imagined. I learned suffering is always an invitation to turn to God and discover that He truly is sufficient.

Regardless of where you are in your journey of suffering, my prayer is that you will lean into Jesus and find that He is more than enough to meet all your needs. I'm praying that:

- God's love will be so real, personal, and life-giving that He fills you to overflowing with His presence.

- Your prayer life won't be solely about asking God for what you need but will include resting and delighting in Him, knowing you are His beloved.

- You will trust in God's unfailing love and His promise to provide all you need, even when you don't understand what is happening.

Stop for a minute, and consider where you were when we first began, what was on your mind, and what you were hoping for.

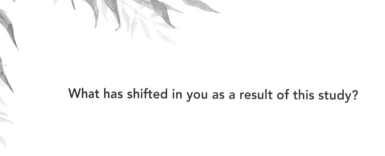

What has shifted in you as a result of this study?

Where have you seen your trust in the Lord grow? How has He spoken to you? How have you been changed? Journal your thoughts.

If you were explaining to a good friend what you've learned from this Bible study, what would you say?

WHAT IF THIS NEVER GETS BETTER?

Watch the Session 7 video and take notes below.

GROUP DISCUSSION / QUESTIONS FOR REFLECTION

What part of the video teaching was most significant for you? Why?

Is it possible to have hope and joy even in the midst of chronic or terminal suffering? How?

Why is keeping eternity in our sights so important as we suffer?

Why do we focus so much time and energy on this life when it is so short? How can we live more for eternity than this temporal life?

How has your view of suffering been affected by what you've learned today?

What are some important takeaways from this study?

How has this study equipped you to walk through your own suffering and to help others in their trials?

To access the video teaching sessions, use the instructions in the back of your Bible study book.

BEFORE YOU GO . . . MY HEART FOR YOU

We've journeyed together through a lot of emotional topics and questions, haven't we? Thank you for sticking with me—I'm sure some weeks were hard to process as you dealt with your pain and the pain of the people around you. I pray as you reflect on what you've learned that your burdens feel lighter, and God feels nearer.

I've loved walking with you through this study, sharing what God has taught me in suffering. I've even loved sharing parts of my crazy Christmas letters! I'm hoping that the framework I outlined, the 3 Ps I cling to in pain, will anchor you in God as you weather your own suffering. Experiencing God's presence, knowing my pain has a purpose, and trusting in the promise of heaven gave me courage and confidence when life felt crushingly difficult—and they continue to do so.

If you're in a season of suffering, you may feel alone and afraid, as if you're in a terrifying freefall and don't know how it will end. You may wonder what's safe and what you can rely on. But you may also have discovered that when everything certain is stripped away, your suffering story is God's love story for you. He is teaching you to be aware of His presence and to rely on Him, which is easier to do when what you once relied on is gone.

The promise of heaven, knowing your suffering will end in glory, can sustain you through unspeakable pain. We long for the unending delight of heaven when we will experience unbroken communion and fellowship with God, beholding His glory, becoming lost in His presence. The incredible news is that those are all available to you now—you just need to be aware of God's invitation.

The Lord is inviting you to find your joy in Him, and not in your circumstances. You may find that joy in stillness and silence, as you sense God's love surrounding you. You may find it as you read Scripture, as the words come to life before your eyes. You may find it in the realization that God really is meeting all your needs, and you lack nothing.

I love Isaiah's words to the Israelites which can be yours as well: "The LORD will guide you continually and satisfy your desire in scorched places and make your bones strong; and you shall be like a watered garden, like a spring of water, whose waters do not fail" (Isa. 58:11). God alone can satisfy your desires in scorched places with His living water—your inner life can blossom in the desert.

I'm praying that you will discover all those things for yourself. That you'll find an unshakable joy as you sense God's presence and see everything in your life as purposeful. That you'll trust God is working for your good, shaping you through your suffering, and that it will end in glory. It'll all be worth it. I promise. You are beloved.

With love and hope,

DIFFICULT MOMENTS AND LOW POINTS IN MY LIFE

Jot down the challenges you are facing right now—the pain, grief, fears, loss, and longings. Next, add the hardest events and lowest points of your life with approximate dates.

Finding out the reason for Ken's BP plunges

HAPPY MOMENTS AND HIGH POINTS IN MY LIFE

Write a list of the best and happiest moments in your life. Capture all the seasons you would consider "high points" in your life. Include approximate dates as well.

My TIME LINE

HAPPY MOMENTS

BIRTH

DIFFICULT MOMENTS

CURRENT AGE

ENDNOTES

SESSION 2

1. Douglas K. Stuart, *Exodus, vol. 2, The New American Commentary* (Nashville: Broadman & Holman Publishers, 2006), 705.

2. Strong's Greek: 3767, οὖν (oun), *Englishman's Concordance*, accessed November 21, 2022, https://biblehub.com/greek/strongs_3767.htm.

3. Craig S. Keener, *The IVP Bible Background Commentary: New Testament* (Downers Grove, IL: InterVarsity Press, 1993), Jn 11:20.

4. Strong's Greek: 1690, ἐμβριμάομαι Embrimaomai, *Strong's Concordance, Englishman's Concordance*, https://biblehub.com/greek/1690.htm.

5. Tim Keller, "Tim Keller's Sermon After 9/11," *The Gospel Coalition*, September 11, 2021, https://www.thegospelcoalition.org/article/tim-kellers-sermon-9-11/.

6. Strong's Greek: 1145, δακρύω dakruó, *Strong's Concordance*, https://biblehub.com/greek/1145.htm.

7. John F. MacArthur Jr., *John 1–11, MacArthur New Testament Commentary* (Chicago: Moody Press, 2006), 461–462.

8. Joni Eareckson Tada, *A Place of Healing* (Colorado Springs: David C. Cook, 2010), 35.

9. Christa Wells, "Held," Natalie Grant's *Awaken* album, 2005.

10. Emily Velasco, "Ultrafast Camera Takes 1 Trillion Frames Per Second of Transparent Objects and Phenomena," *Caltech*, January 17, 2020, https://www.caltech.edu/about/news/ultrafast-camera-takes-1-trillion-frames-second-transparent-objects-and-phenomena#:~:text=A%20little%20over%20a%20year,being%20quick%20is%20not%20enough.

11. Strong's G1097: ginóskó, *Strong's Concordance*, https://biblehub.com/greek/1097.htm/.

12. "Beloved Is Where We Begin" (excerpt) © Jan Richardson from *Circle of Grace: A Book of Blessings for the Seasons*. Used by permission. janrichardson.com

13. Elisabeth Elliot, *Quest for Love* (Grand Rapids: Revell, 1996), ebook, ch. 19.

14. Elisabeth Elliot, *Finding Your Way Through Loneliness* (Grand Rapids: Revell, 2011), ebook, ch. 4.

SESSION 3

1. Strong's H7879: *śîaḥ, Blue Letter Bible*, https://www.blueletterbible.org/lexicon/h7879/esv/wlc/0-1/
Strong's H3708: *ka'as, Blue Letter Bible*, https://www.blueletterbible.org/lexicon/h3708/kjv/wlc/0-1/

2. "The Chinese Bamboo Tree—Les Brown Motivational Speech," *Motivation Mentalist*, July 23, 2018, https://motivationmentalist.com/?s=chinese+bamboo+tree.

3. John Piper, *Reading the Bible Supernaturally* (Wheaton: Crossway, 2017), ebook.

SESSION 4

1. Elisabeth Elliot, *Suffering is Never for Nothing* (Nashville: B&H Publishing Group, 2019), ebook, ch. 3.

2. Vaneetha Risner, "What if the Worst Happens?" *Desiring God*, September 15, 2014, https://www.desiringgod.org/articles/what-if-the-worst-happens.

3. Michael J. Wilkins, *Matthew, The NIV Application Commentary* (Grand Rapids, MI: Zondervan Publishing House, 2004), 517.

4. Tim Keller (@timkellerynyc), "The peace of God is not the absence of fear. It, in fact, is his presence," *Twitter*, October 20, 20202, 1:23 p.m., https://twitter.com/timkellerynyc/status/1318618738804035584?lang=en.

5. Paul Tripp, "What You Need to Know about Suffering," *paultripp.com*, October 3, 2018, https://www.paultripp.com/wednesdays-word/posts/what-you-need-to-know-about-suffering.

SESSION 5

1. C. S. Lewis, *A Grief Observed* (New York: Harper Collins, 1961), Ebook, Ch. 3.

2. "3 P's," *Growing Resilient*, accessed November 30, 2022, https://growingresilient.com/home/tools/3-ps/.

3. Evelyn Christensen, *What Happens When Women Pray* (Wheaton: Victor Books, 1991, 89–90.

4. C. H. Spurgeon, "Woe and Weal (No. 3239)," Metropolitan Tabernacle, March 2, 1911, https://ccel.org/ccel/spurgeon/sermons57/sermons57.ix.html.

5. Joni Eareckson Tada, *When God Weeps* (Grand Rapids: Zondervan, 1997), 84.

6. Ibid, ch. 6

7. John Piper, "God Is Always Doing 10,000 Things in Your Life," *Desiring God*, January 1, 2013, https://www.desiringgod.org/articles/god-is-always-doing-10000-things-in-your-life.

8. John Newton, "Letter 4, London, Aug. 19, 1775," *The Letters of John Newton*, Monergism Books, 628, https://www.monergism.com/thethreshold/sdg/newton/The_Letters_of_John_Newton_-_John_Newton.pdf.

9. Paul Tripp, "I Wish God Acted Earlier," paultripp.com, March 30, 2022, https://www.paultripp.com/wednesdays-word/posts/i-wish-god-acted-earlier.

SESSION 6

1. J. Daniel Hays and J. Scott Duvall, eds., *The Baker Illustrated Bible Handbook* (Grand Rapids, MI: Baker Books, 2011), 204.

2. John Piper, "Job: Reverent in Suffering," desiringgod.org, July 7, 1985, https://www.desiringgod.org/messages/job-reverent-in-suffering

SESSION 7

1. K. A. Mathews, *Genesis 11:27–50:26, vol. 1B, The New American Commentary* (Nashville: Broadman & Holman Publishers, 2005), 467.

2. Paula Rinehart, *Better Than My Dreams* (Nashville, Thomas Nelson, 2007), 179.

3. John Piper (@JohnPiper), "Occasionally weep deeply over the life you hoped would be. Grieve the losses. Then wash your face. Trust God. And embrace the life you have," *Twitter*, March 1, 2016, 7:04 a.m., https://twitter.com/johnpiper/status/704653441533132800?lang=en.

4. David Jeremiah, *Hope: Living Fearlessly in a Scary World* (Carol Stream: Tyndale Momentum, 2021), 181.

5. Thomas R. Schreiner, *1, 2 Peter, Jude, vol. 37, The New American Commentary* (Nashville: Broadman & Holman Publishers, 2003), 67.

6. J. R. R. Tolkien, *The Return of the King* (New York: Harper Collins, 1967), 283.

7. C. S. Lewis, *The Great Divorce* (New York: Harper Collins, 1946), 69.

8. Randy Alcorn, "Looking Forward to a Heaven We Can Imagine," Eternal Perspective Ministries, October 30, 2016, https://www.epm.org/blog/2016/Oct/30/looking-forward-heaven-we-can-imagine.

9. Ibid.

10. Quoted in E.M. Bounds, *Heaven: A Place, A City, A Home* (Grand Rapids: Baker Book House, 1975), p.13.

11. Elisabeth Elliot, *Made for the Journey* (Grand Rapids: Revell, 1998), ebook, preface.

12. C. S. Lewis, *Till We Have Face*, (Harvest/HBJ, 1956), 308.

13. Ron Deal, *The Smart Stepfamily* (Bloomington: Bethany House Publishers, 2014), 52.

Get the most from your study.

IN THIS STUDY, YOU'LL:

- Gain confidence to bring your hard questions to God.
- Find strength and hope through Scripture when all hope seems lost.
- Be equipped to come alongside others who are suffering.
- Rest in the presence, purposes, and promises of God.
- Reframe your circumstances in light of the bigger story.

To enrich your study experience, consider the accompanying video teaching sessions, approximately 10–20 minutes, from Vaneetha Risner.

STUDYING ON YOUR OWN?

Watch Vaneetha Risner's teaching sessions, available via redemption code for individual video-streaming access, printed in this Bible study book.

LEADING A GROUP?

Each group member will need a *Desperate for Hope* Bible Study Book, which includes video access. Because all participants will have access to the video content, you can choose to watch the videos outside of your group meeting if desired. Or, if you're watching together and someone misses a group meeting, she'll have the flexibility to catch up! A DVD set is also available to purchase separately if desired.

COMPANION PRODUCT

DVD set, includes 7 video teaching sessions from Vaneetha Risner, each approximately 10–20 minutes

FREE RESOURCES AVAILABLE ONLINE

Desperate for Hope Scripture Document

Because this study features many Scripture references, we've provided a downloadable document that contains the full text of every Scripture referenced in the study.

You can find this document at lifeway.com/desperateforhope.

Leader Guide

This downloadable document will help the leader prepare to lead the study and provide instruction for the content and flow of each group session.

You'll find this document at lifeway.com/desperateforhope.

Browse study formats, a free session sample, leader guide, video clips, church promotional materials, and more at

lifeway.com/desperateforhope